Infinite Refuge

Other Works by Virgil Suárez

Fiction:

The Cutter
Latin Jazz
Havana Thursdays
Going Under
Welcome to the Oasis, a novella & stories

Memoir:

Spared Angola:
Memories From a Cuban-American Childhood

Poetry:

You Come Singing
Garabato Poems
In the Republic of Longing
Palm Crows
Banyan
Guide to the Blue Tongue

Anthologies:

Iguana Dreams: New Latino Fiction
Paper Dance: 55 Latino Poets
Little Havana Blues: A Contemporary
Cuban-American Literature Anthology
Is There a Boom in Latino Literature?
American Diaspora: Poetry of Exile
Like Thunder: Poets Respond to Violence in America
Clockpunchers: Poetry of the Workplace
Micro 2: Really Short Fiction

Infinite Refuge

by

Virgil Suárez

Arte Público Press
Houston, Texas

This volume is made possible through grants from the City of Houston through The Cultural Arts Council of Houston, Harris County.

Recovering the past, creating the future

Arte Público Press
University of Houston
452 Cullen Performance Hall
Houston, Texas 77204-2004

Cover design by Giovanni Mora.
Cover art courtesy of Luis Cruz Azaceta, "The Immigrant" 1985.

Suárez, Virgil, 1962–.
　Infinite Refuge / Virgil Suárez.
　　　p.　cm.
　　ISBN 1-55885-348-0 (pbk. : alk. paper)
　　1. Suárez, Virgil, 1962–　2. Authors, American—20th century—Biography.　3. Suárez, Virgil, 1962—Family.
4. Cuban Americans—Biography.　5. Cuban American families.　I. Title.
PS3569.U18 Z75 2002
813'.54—dc21
[B]　　　　　　　　　　　　　　　　　　2002066673
　　　　　　　　　　　　　　　　　　　　　CIP

∞ The paper used in this publication meets the requirements of the American National Standard for Information Sciences—Permanence of Paper for Printed Library Materials, ANSI Z39.48-1984.

2 3 4 5 6 7 8 9 0 1　　　　　10 9 8 7 6 5 4 3 2 1

For Dr. Nicolás Kanellos
friend, editor, teacher.

Contents

Acknowledgments

Grateful acknowledgment is made to the editors and publishers of the following reviews and journals where some of these pieces first appeared, sometimes in a slightly different form:

American Literary Review, Another Chicago Magazine, Artful Dodge, The Bloomsbury Review, Boulevard, The Caribbean Writer, Cimarron, Clackamas Literary Review, Colorado Review, Connecticut Review, Crab Orchard Review, Crazyhorse, The Florida Review, Fourteen Hills: The SFSU Review, Hawaii Review, Hopscotch, Indiana Review, Luna, Mid-American Review, New England Review, The Patterson Literary Review, Prairie Schooner, Shenandoah, Sycamore Review, Tameme, TriQuarterly, Water & Stone, and *Zone 3.*

Several of these pieces were nominated by the editors of the magazines in which they first appeared for a Pushcart Prize.

I would like to thank the staff of Arte Público Press for all the years of support and loyalty, in particular, my editor and publisher Nicolás Kanellos. Great thanks go to Marina Tristán, one of the great ladies of publishing, and to the great staff that makes Arte Público Press a wonderful family, too.

An individual artist grant from the Florida State Arts Council helped tremendously in the completion of this book.

Entre la noche y el mar,
está la isla.

Entre el desespero y la distancia,
está el hombre.

Entre el hombre y la isla,
está el recuerdo.

Y también el refugio infinito.

Between the night and the sea,
this island.

Between despair and distance,
this man.

Between this man and this island,
this remembrance.

And also an infinite refuge.

Balsero Dreams

I confess not the obvious. I don't care much for television. The last news story I watched unfold in its entirety was the O. J. Simpson chase down the Harbor Freeway in Los Angeles. My eyes kept watering because I wouldn't blink, that's how fixed on the screen I was. I kept asking myself why I continued to watch, but it was to look at all the people lined up by the sides of the highway, holding placards of support for their once-running-back hero. That was long ago.

This year I'm in Key Biscayne, Florida, on vacation, when my mother calls me from Hialeah to tell me to turn on the television. "*Mira eso*," she tells me, screaming her words into the phone as usual. I ask her in Spanish what, what is going on?

"Turn on the television," she says, "and you will see the disaster that Cuba is!"

And I'm thinking, what in the world could have happened? What does my mother know that I don't? I missed the Tiananmen Square showdown between the Chinese university student and the tank. I missed the fall of the Berlin Wall. I missed all of Monica Lewinsky, President Clinton's videotaped deposition. It seems I've missed most of televised contemporary world history. But I read the newspaper. *The New York Times* is enough for me. *The Miami Herald* for the hometown news.

My wife and I had gone to see the Wim Wenders' documentary about the Buena Vista Social Club, and both my wife and I were blown away by the decay of Old Havana—it didn't look like the grand city at all (of years past, maybe in 1959),

1

but Kosovo or Baghdad, something war-torn, reduced to rubble. Maybe someone put a bomb somewhere in *La Habana Vieja*, all those historical buildings, and there–KABOOM!—went the city, not too far-fetched, I thought, remembering last summer's news about the serial bombings in Havana.

"Channel 23," she tells me, "it's on the news. Hurry!"

And I run from the balcony where I had been sitting looking out at the Key Biscayne waters (Cuba is ninety miles from Key West, the southernmost point of the United States) to the bedroom, turn on the television, fumble with the channel changer, and there . . . Channel 23 . . . a raft afloat in the wake of these waves made by a coastguard helicopter. The small, flimsy boat is surrounded by a couple of coastguard cutters and a launch. There are men on the makeshift vessel, almost naked except for their tattered shorts.

A couple jump in the water because the men on the coastguard launch are trying to reel them in.

I tell my mother I'll call her later, and before I hang up, I hear her shout: "*Esos pobres diablos, mira eso . . .*" Those poor devils, look at them.

They are trying to push themselves and their boat-raft away from the hull of the bigger ships, then one of the men on the coastguard launch squirts pepper spray into the eyes of the Cuban rafters. The men turn away, a couple more jump in the water.

Those already in the water begin to swim toward shore. They are not too far from making the beach in Surfside. The newscaster says they are trying to make it to United States soil—only then will they not be sent back.

Every time they swim—their desperate attempts to keep their heads afloat—the coastguard helicopter turns downward to blast them away on the wake-waves that the helicopter blades make. It's a lose-lose situation.

People gather to cheer the Cubans on. Tourists. Beachcombers. Some Cuban Americans, some Canadian snowbirds. People from the heartland.

I am now sitting down in the sunlit room, not believing my eyes. I mean, all this is happening not too far from me. I'm almost tempted to look out the window toward Surfside in Miami Beach. The television brings continuous images of the swimmers trying to make it.

When the first two Cuban rafters swim ashore, there are a couple of policemen there to arrest them. The men spot them and play chase-and-tag first. The crowds go wild now, some Cuban-American men and women boo and hiss, try to get in the way of the policemen and the exhausted swimmers. Everybody is red in the face from screaming, shouting. The cops cringe because they are seeing their authority challenged. Two policemen work one *balsero* on to his stomach and handcuff him, as another officer tries to keep the circle of men and women from coming in too close. They are exchanging words, not pretty ones from the looks on their angry faces.

This is all being televised from the air, for the most part. And back on the water the coastguard is still trying to bring the boat in or sink it. It's amazing. My eyes start to water again, this time from both not blinking and because I, too, am feeling the rage. When the men continue to refuse to board the coastguard boat, the men on the coastguard cutter, driven mad by so much of their inability to control the situation, now try to ram the boat into sinking.

Don't they know they are being watched? Filmed? This is going on the record, no? I ask myself. Don't they see this is going to come back to haunt them?

I still can't believe my eyes. Now the Cuban radio stations are going crazy, too. They are telling the story over the air, and Cubans on their way home from work stop traffic on the McArthur Causeway, the link between the beaches and the mainland. All traffic stops. A man steps out of his car and unfolds a huge Cuban flag over himself as he lies down in the middle of the road. Nobody is going anywhere. Boats begin to appear. There's madness everywhere, on the streets, on the water.

When the men are finally overpowered and taken away, Miami Beach, some parts of Dade County, and Hialeah (Hialeah, in particular, because it is almost 70 percent Cuban) shut down. People are on the streets with picket signs, demonstrating; the police get ready. Soon enough, the director of the coastguard in Miami appears in a news conference. He tells the people that the coastguard made a mistake, it should not have behaved as it did.

People wanted to know about the fate of the Cuban rafters, and he announced that for the time being they would not be sent back.

It is a lot easier to write about this now. I sat there and lost track of time. My mother-in-law and my wife would come in to check on the development of the story, which after a while the news channels simply stopped replaying to bring on the news pundits.

Lincoln Díaz-Balart, a Cuban-American congressman, called on the Clinton administration to suspend its 1995 immigration accord with Cuba. "This administration's policy is immoral," he said. "It can no longer continue to sweep the Cuban crisis under the carpet. The Cuban crisis and the tragedy of oppression of the Cuban people must no longer be treated as an immigration issue."

I remember my father, dead two years now, discussing the 1995 agreement, which was created out of "a sense of urgency and pragmatism" resulting from an influx of nearly 30,000 Cuban refugees during the summer of 1994. Under the terms of the accord, the United States agreed to issue 20,000 visas for Cubans to immigrate legally to the United States, but to repatriate Cubans picked up at sea. Not those who set foot on land. And I recalled my mother-in-law every once in a while calling us in Tallahassee, where my family and I live, to inform us that more Cubans had been smuggled onto U.S. shores, practically dropped off behind La Carreta Restaurant in Key Biscayne.

One boatload of Cubans reached shore on the property of singer Jimmy Buffet in one of the lower keys one summer. A doctor and his family, all dressed in wet suits. They apparently expected rough seas, so they dressed for it. How they procured those scuba outfits they never told.

"These Cubans," my mother-in-law told us, "do not look like malnourished, weather-beaten rafters. These men, women, and children looked merely windswept as they suddenly appeared here."

And I ask, why do they keep coming?

Even after the Mariel Exodus, which began in May of 1980, after the Peruvian Embassy storm-in in Havana. Jimmy Carter was president. I was about to graduate from high school, living in Los Angeles, the son of two blue-collar workers who had taken me out of Cuba to, as my maternal grandmother once put it, "spare me Angola." My parents didn't want to see their only child drafted into the military and then be sent off to be killed in some revolution in Africa. They were nonpolitical people, hard workers looking for a better life.

Forty years of communism has left the people of Cuba little choice, especially the young people. I don't blame them for wanting to get out, by any means necessary, even if it means on a raft. And most of them know the odds of making the perilous journey from the island to *Los Estados Unidos*. One out of every four. I have this written by my computer at home.

They want freedom—every one of them who makes it tells the newspapers, radio stations—freedom not only to say what they want, but to dress any way they want, play whatever music they like, travel without constantly being asked where they are going. These are the simple givens we take for granted here in the United States on a daily basis.

It is the lure of possibility and a graspable future that blinds so many into crossing. Most of them don't make it, as they either drown, get killed by the Cuban coastguard, or are eaten by sharks. I've heard the stories, all too often, as everyone does. It's a body count kept mostly in Miami by Cubans, not only by families who lose members, but by those who refuse to forget.

A few years ago when the issue of the *balseros* or rafters made national news with the summer of 1994 record-breaking arrivals, a raft collector set up a display of these vessels on his front lawn. That way, people could drive by and stop and see for themselves how the *balseros* brave the Florida Straits—a definite homage to the ingenuity of the desperate and determined to be free. Also a viewable testament to the act of leaving.

My wife and I drove by and stopped to look. The whole lawn was littered with these inner tubes, Styrofoam and wood floats, Royal Palm tree dugouts (like when the Taínos and Arawak traveled their once-idyllic island), practically anything that could float, invented vessels that only someone crazy and desperate enough would climb aboard to float the ninety miles to the Keys.

Of course, there were the tales of the man who came to Miami in a Cadillac converted into a boat in the early sixties, and when he arrived, the story goes, the automobile manufacturer gave him a brand-new one. Then there was the sixteen-year-old who came over a couple of summers ago, so he said, on a wind surfer. His story captured my imagination because I could see this kid, out on the water everyday practicing, waiting for the right wind patterns, and then off he went. Hollywood even talked about buying the rights to make a movie out of it, but of course who would sit for two hours to watch this kid wind surf over?

I read about and lived with that story long enough to finally write something about it. A poem. Not entirely about what leads a teenage boy to such a crazy act because recently it seems many teenage boys are driven to madness by everything around them, but, well, other reasons. Here is the poem:

Lament for the Boy Rafter (A *Balsero*'s Dream)

everyday on his way to school he stops briefly to sniff
the sea air, looks toward the horizon in the distance,

looks at the wind-swept coconut palm fronds, their flicker
of light, and on his way home to the clapboard, makeshift

hut, he looks at the cracks on the ground, counts pebbles,
picks up twigs, broken pieces of wood, fallen branches,

he reads their knobby joints, splintered ridges, like some language
of the depraved, walks home slowly, nowhere to go fast,

and everyday he daydreams of how wood floats on water,
the good, light kind the currents can take far, far away

from this broken island, he tells his sisters, his brother,
his mother, not to wait up for him if one day he doesn't come

back, and they laugh at him, this skinny boy of nine, green
eyes, green spirit, and at night, in the waking of all things lost,

he dreams of boats, pieces of wood, an inner tube, black circles
on the water, all lined up from Santiago to Miami, and he skips

from one tube to another, a child's game, his only way out.

It is only when you look at one of these makeshift rafts up close that you feel the journey, the way canvas and rope netting is tied to a Russian-built truck inner tube big enough to float with three or four people. The scratch marks and weathering tell the story best. They are a dictionary of longing, a map of the lost, testament to why people offer their lives in the ultimate act of leaving.

We are all essentially leavers. I remember the act of leaving Cuba once. I still vividly recall the specifics: a big suitcase, my mother cutting the curtains down and sewing them into liners for the suitcase; my father, who smoked in those days, stepping out onto the porch of his house, our house, bought in the mid-fifties on his policeman's salary, smoke clouds in front of him, clouds tangled by the fronds of the plantains that touched the porch columns. I was almost eight years old, a child looking up at his father in a reflective, vulnerable moment for the first time.

He kept pacing in and out, this would be the last time he would put out his cigarette on our porch. He told us it was time to go, and I saw the resolution in his moist eyes. The anxiety had turned his hands into birds.

"*Listo*," he told us. Ready, it was time to leave, and I heard my father say "*adios vieja*," toward the room where my grandmother had died, as though she was still there and we were simply leaving on a short vacation trip, and I knew better. We all did.

I must have fallen asleep in the taxi, which was no taxi but the car of Talo, our next-door neighbor who gave us a ride to the airport. The next thing I opened my eyes to was the entrance to the José Martí Rancho Boyeros Airport and a few relatives waiting to say good-bye. How they got there from so far away, I'll never know, other than family calls to family. Everyone knew what I didn't, which was that it was the last time, the last time for my father who died in exile, never again to be in his homeland, the last time for me who keeps his son-promise not to go back until . . .

In a damaged country, people learn to sacrifice, learn how to say good-bye, and mean it sometimes.

We were finally on our way out. At last. To Madrid, Spain. The nuns in the family provided visas for us—them and my paternal uncle who sent the dollars for all the application and processing fees.

Next I remembered the hallway, all the glass they call *la pecera*, the fish tank, because once you are in, you cannot touch your relatives, but you can see them and they you. My maternal grandmother Donatila stood behind the glass, already a specter. My uncles and aunts, cousins, all learned to wave good-bye. As if in a trance, we waved back and boarded the plane—I think it was a Cubana Airlines jet, its doors the gateway to freedom, as my father said. (I remember my father letting out a big sigh of relief as though he knew that as soon as the plane took off from Cuban soil, we were all free). This was the first time I was to fly.

Sitting in silence, my mother leaned into my father's shoulders and cried. I gripped the armrest, a boy of no more than forty-five pounds, and saw the way my fingers dug into the thin padding. When the plane took off, the silence, I'm sure, made the ascension possible, a steel bird weighed down with so much melancholy, so much sadness, so much nostalgia. My father looked out the window and smiled.

(This is in no way meant as a comparison between our simple and easy leaving and those of the *balseros*.)

Cubans share an obsession with departures, with leaving, whether they are saying a daily good-bye or traveling far, where they will stay for years. I have not seen the family I left behind in Cuba, all my uncles, aunts, cousins, and my maternal grandfather, in almost thirty years.

Distance has made me extra sensitive about leaving places, saying good-bye. Departures frighten me now. They make me anxious and leery, and it isn't that my responsibilities have doubled with a wife and a couple of daughters. No. It is the gap of space and time. The physical separation, the not being around in their own lives where they can see me, make contact—perhaps it is what my analyst once certified: that I had a deep fear of death and dying. The sole reason why I had so much trouble with going away was not being there with the family. Were all those panic attacks rooted in this truth?

I still simply ask: who wouldn't feel detached? Separated? Gone?

I always travel with great reluctance, always looking out of airplane windows at the ground, those beautiful patches of green and brown earth—the physicalness of being rooted. I think that this is precisely what the *balseros* rely upon to keep up their courage, except instead of the ground, they must rely upon the water, the connector between these two shores of exile. The transition is made that much more fluid and constancy is the propellant.

The morning we left Cuba, I looked out at the lights of the distant homeland, a flicker and wink of lights saying good-bye, for the last time, and we were soaring through the air toward the unknown. So much left behind, and I, I too, have learned this intricate art of leaving, of saying good-bye to everything that is home, memories like fire, a leaver's good-bye to all things irretrievable. Our leaving took place in November of 1970.

I imagine what rafters must see for such a long time during their own leaving, this same flicker and fading of distant lights (green, I think, like the lights Jay Gatsby succumbed to as he looked out at the shores of West Egg in Fitzgerald's novel *The Great Gatsby*) as the sun rises upon them for the first time.

Another reason why Cubans might be so obsessed with leaving and departing has to do with the fact that they do it all too often, always with the great insecurity of a nonreturn. For many of us there hasn't been a return yet, though most of us are going back now to "visit" Cuba. Those old ghosts of places we knew, lived in—moments we survived—those are the things I'm afraid of.

Often, when asked at readings on college and university campuses why I don't go back to Cuba (a question I take with the utmost seriousness) I simply say that I don't want to renounce my American citizenship, which if you were born in Cuba and you return to the island, you must do. The Cuban government doesn't recognize the American citizenship of Cubans born on the island, and though you don't renounce it for good, who would want to? Not me.

The real reason (if there are real reasons left) is that the getting there, as easy and as rich an experience as other people paint it, the leaving and departing from my family again would break me open like a dam. My family here, and all my extended family there. I would not be able to take the pressure of leaving and saying good-bye again, or too easily. My emotional stability might cease to exist, not that I have much left to speak of.

When my father-in-law got sick with lung cancer and he ended up dying at the hospital in Miami, I sat with him a couple of times, holding his hand and looking into his eyes while his respirator tick-tocked air into his lungs. He was gone, it seemed, under the heavy-duty doses of morphine. A couple of times, I saw a flicker in his eyes that to this day I believe was him saying good-bye to me. My own father passed away a year later in 1997. He went into the hospital to have cancer removed from his colon, survived the surgery, but during the last moments of recovery, on the day he was supposed to come home, a blood clot traveled to his heart and killed him. I remember I didn't get a chance to say good-bye because the Code Blue team didn't want me to see how they ripped open his chest cavity to massage his heart.

Departing and saying good-bye, knowing that there is no return from a long journey is, I believe, always too much for the human heart. I know I have a melancholic streak in me, but when you look into the eyes of a dead person, you can see the darkened pupils, a curtain closed forever to those living, as if they speak a "you shall find no more answers to life in exile here."

Now as a grown man, a working writer, a professor on his summer break, I always travel with my family down from Tallahassee to Key Biscayne and Hialeah, where we spend time with my mother and mother-in-law. I usually reserve the summer to work on my writing. For seven years now I've been working on a novel about a man who leaves Cuba and never returns. A famous musician who, as the story goes, was so popular he left his music to fight in Sierra Maestra because he thought that it was his duty and responsibility, that his fame and notoriety would help the rebels' cause, then quickly saw the Revolution for what it really was, and left the island. He was also a black man in love with a high-society white woman whose father didn't approve of their love, and who had taken out a contract on the musician's life, but that's another story now.

Or I write poems. Mostly though, I find myself reading books about Cuba and Cuban affairs, the newspapers on Cuban matters and gossip, what my father called *El Politiqueo.*

I swim, I spend time with my two daughters, who've learned how to swim during these summer trips. I think about my dead father and dead father-in-law. I think morbid thoughts because the cemeteries of Miami are filling up with people who left their homeland and never returned, not even as a dying wish. (The offshore waters devour one out of every four Cuban rafters, and the remains of their failed journeys wash upon the shores of the Keys all the time.) Usually, the summer also goes following stories about the rafters, the *balseros* who brave the dangerous currents and weather of the Florida Straits to come to the United States.

The Cuban community keeps track of the numbers every summer. So does the U.S. Immigration Department. It has been a rocky recent history, with Cuban rafters being caught on high seas and returned, an act that angers the exiled Cubans. It angers me, too, because I've never understood why we need to guard our borders. After all, this is the richest country in the world.

More than ever, border-guarding and keeping has become a national obsession and pastime. We are driven to silliness (not to say pure evil) by this crazy notion that if we guard our border and keep people out, the rest of the world will not come here to steal our jobs. What jobs? Cleaning toilets like my mother did for fifteen years, sewing zippers on denim jeans at piecemeal wages, picking vegetables and fruit, factory work like my father, doing the grunt work on roadside constructions? Which jobs are we afraid these immigrants will steal from us?

But I promise this is an essay about the elementals of leaving, of saying final good-byes, and not a political diatribe. I've never considered myself a political person, writer, whatever. For the most part, I let my fiction and poetry speak for itself. I write about people, their lives, their departures and arrivals, focusing mainly on the anxieties of their leaving. I wrote an entire novel about this called *The Cutter*. The story is about a young man so blinded by his desires to leave the island that he decides to cross the Florida Straits at any cost. Oh, and how it costs him.

Everybody loses—that's my motto these days when I see injustices done to people who cross borders, not only on the ground, but on water. We are continuing our terrible history of border atrocities between the United States and Mexico.

No, I like to leave the political things for the pundits, the know-it-alls, and God knows there are plenty of those everywhere. I'm simply interested in movement, in arrivals and departures, saying good-bye, but not forever. All this coming and going between Cubans on the island and Cubans in exile is enough to make anyone dizzy. I remember arguing with my father about why my mother wanted (needed) to go back: so she could see her mother alive one last time, so she can feel rooted again. In fact, for many years I've been envious of all those who go back. But I also made a promise to my father I wouldn't go back until change arrived on Cuban soil. All I have left is my work, the daily writing, the harvesting of memories. Memories such as how we left Cuba for Spain in the fall of 1970 . . .

We made a refueling stop in the Azores, and for the first time I saw a toy store. We spent about a two-hour layover at the airport, and at the duty-free shop they had toys behind the glass. Little Matchbox cars, the wink of polished chrome hypnotizing me. My parents always remind me that they left Cuba with nothing but me. Nothing else. No clothes, no money, no other belongings. (What was in that one suitcase I remembered?)

I remember the coats that my father had bartered a few rabbits and chickens for. Wooly black coats for the three of us. My mother has a picture taken a couple of years later in those same coats when we left Spain for the United States. Certainly, we looked like three warm and cozy penguins.

Immediately after the *balseros* arrive and are taken to the Krome immigration facilities in South Florida, after they are fed and given clothes, after they are allowed to rest for a couple of days, they begin to look different, alive, energized by the prospects of freedom and possibility.

I often tell my daughters the story of my childhood because something in me refuses to forget, to let them take the goods and comforts that surround them for granted. *Si solamente supieran*, if they only knew, my mother will often remind me, just in case I've forgotten, the fact that we came to this country with nothing.

I share with them these stories of the *balseros*, of their swimming to shore to live free. Of their waving good-bye to their families, to strangers and onlookers waving awkward good-byes, as if to say more than a mere "take good care, *adiós*."

We swim in the pool. In the ocean. I tell them to imagine how hard the swimming would be if they were stranded in the middle of nowhere, if all they could see and feel was water. Then even the sky is a mirror of the sea, a reflection of what the water takes, gives back.

No matter what laws are imposed, no matter what happens, this is what I know: as long as the Cuban people don't have human rights and the kinds of freedom we enjoy here in the United States, there will be those desperate and driven to try their luck on the water. Simple.

Lucky are those who make it.

The way these men arrive on the shores of Miami Beach, naked, sunburned and emaciated. The only thing still alive in them is the belief that they will now live free. They can now look at the water and not long for it. In the same way it must be that we find our own ways home after so much leaving, after so many good-byes.

Mine is a culture of leaving. We must all learn slowly to live with the finality and uncertainty of departure.

Gusano at the Hatuey Brewery

The government placed my father in a job at the Hatuey Brewery not too far from where we lived in Arroyo Naranjo. The brewery was named after the great Siboney Indian chief who stood up against the Spanish and was burned at the stake. As the story goes, the Indian chief turned down heaven because when he asked if the Spanish would also go there, the priest said yes. Hatuey responded that he'd rather die and go to hell. My father started as a bottle cleaner, then a packer, and before long he sat in front of fluorescent lights and inspected the clean bottles before they were filled with beer or *malta* (a hops-and-malt soft drink) as they passed by on a conveyor belt.

He labored twelve hours a day, sometimes volunteering on Saturdays because he didn't want trouble anymore—he had already been arrested twice for counterrevolutionary activities, which my grandmother and mother denied. If anything, my father lived with a short fuse for being called names like *escoria* and *gusano*—the first meant *trash* and the other *worm, maggot*. He simply yearned to be able to leave the island for Spain with his family.

My father made many friends at the brewery, and they could drink all the beer they wanted as long as they didn't get drunk on the job. My father drank a lot, developed a prosperous gut my mother made fun of, saying he was getting too fat for his own health, but he liked the beer.

A couple of his friends wanted him to join a smuggling operation to sneak cases of beer out and sell them in the black market, said they'd make lots of money, but my father wanted no trouble. He sat at his post, on a hard wooden stool, and stared at the way light passes through bottles, never sure what he was looking for, maybe stranded roaches or soggy floating cigarettes. Bits of broken glass? Hair? Hypnotized by the sparkle, he daydreamed and thought of his country childhood, when he rode horses all day, fished the lakes for trout, hunted deer, went swimming in the river.

Those days were long gone from his life, and he sat there, lulled numb by the whirring of the conveyor belt. I visited the brewery twice because he wanted me, though only seven (my oldest daughter's age now), to know about hard work. I entered the bowels of the brewery in awe of so much noise: the tinkling of glass hitting glass, metal biting metal, the sound of men over the hissing of the boiling cauldrons where the beer fermented. Pigeons and sparrows made nests high on the I-beams and rafters holding up the roof.

They flew about, shitting on the grease-and-beer-smudged floors. The smell of spoiled beer choked me with its nauseating industry-type smell. Metallic. Like lead vapors. In the penumbra of the huge place, I clung to my father's back pocket. His friends—men with dirty faces and hands, and naked from the waist up—came over, called me *"chamaco,"* kid.

Someone handed me a lukewarm *malta*, which I drank all the time and loved, and said the cold ones were getting colder. Soon I was drinking another, and another, and by midday I could feel and hear the swishing of liquid in my belly, sloshing every time I moved. I sat in the shade and watched my father watch glass. What's the worst thing you've ever found? I asked. "A mouse," he said. *Un ratoncito.* And I thought of a mouse dead in a half-filled bottle, drowned by its own thirst. I kept drinking, and my father warned me it'd give me a stomachache, and so it did. I threw up right there on the floor in front of my feet, a brown liquid, frothy layers of tiny bubbles, long tendrils of mucous hung from my nose. The roar of the men laughing thundered in the brewery. It reverberated all the way around the place, their wicked laughter set the pigeons and sparrows, even the hens incubating eggs, aflutter under the corrugated tin of the roof.

Even today, I will buy a Malta Hatuey in Miami and think back to the roar of those men laughing: ghosts from my father's life, mine, all dead like my father is now. And they are laughing at me, and I love how their laughter turns into a song, glorious, never ending above the sound of glass winking in approval before so much light.

Epidemic

During my last Havana summer, an epidemic broke out all over the island, some German virus that started first in pigs, then infected humans in those nether regions—who knew if they existed—where animals subsisted with humans. No one knew if the rumor of such a disease was true. But one day the Russian-built army trucks arrived, the gravel crunched under such weight through our neighborhood. The armed soldiers spilled out of canvas-tarped backs like grain from a sack, and the bulldozers came and dug huge pits at the corner clearing where people threw trash or abandoned *brujería*-sacrificed animals. Then, while more pits were being dug, the soldiers marched down the streets and house by house, confiscated all the animals in people's patios and yards, one by one, especially the pigs, which squealed like it was the end of the world. And it was. They came and took our six-month piglet. Our Christmas food. They took our rabbits, chickens, even the pet turtle in the cement sink. All the animals were herded toward the corner, in Noah's Ark fashion, to the edge of the pit where they stopped and fought back the precipice. Men with blowtorches set them afire, shot the larger animals like horses and cows and pigs, and simply torched the smaller ones. Chicken and duck feathers burned in midair. Ashes floated in the hot breeze, skyward, rising and falling like leaves.

We gathered at the corner, too afraid of perhaps being next. We children stood by our parents and watched as the animals fell, carcasses charred and burnt to cinders, charred dominos atop each other.

The fires burned for a couple of days and for weeks later, flecks of ashes fell over everything, the smell of flesh, offal, and hide hung thick in the air. Even now, from the distance of thirty years, I can hear the pop and sizzle of fur burning and the talk of fire. I still recall how everything was taken away, except for this burning that lingers in the mind, this torch of resentment, this blackness of remembrance that refuses to be doused.

Fantomas, Master of Disguise

In the mid-sixties, after the Revolution, the movie trucks came to the suburbs in Havana on Saturday nights to show foreign films dubbed in Spanish. Some, like those made in the Soviet Union, were not dubbed, but people watched them anyway. Anything to get out of the heat indoors. The mosquitos rose from the grass and bit our legs. Mine would become infected, and I would spend nights scratching them.

After a long list of bad movies, we, the children, grew restless and started to make noise; fights broke out, food got thrown on the pull-down screen on the side of the movie truck. My father took me to watch this magical film of car chases, caravels lost at sea, camels thirsty in the Egyptian desert, French legionnaires at war on the sand.

And the *Fantomas* films from France, about a master of disguises and masks, was my all-time favorite. No one could ever see his face or know his true identity. Who was this man, half villain, half good guy? British Intelligence was always after him, but he knew a way of hiding, of putting on masks, *disfrazes,* as my father called them, and of getting away in his white car. The car fascinated me because it could travel underwater.

The films were a big hit until people didn't want to get up early Sunday to work in the fields picking potatoes or cabbage. They called it *trabajo voluntario,* volunteer work in the Revolution. It simply meant that after a long week of tiring work at the brewery, Lenin's Park, or the airport, people still had to give something back to the Revolution.

21

One day the films stopped coming, and slowly people gravitated toward the same corner every Saturday night.

The men talking soft, in whispers really.

The women fanning their faces with newspapers.

The children played hide-and-seek, or better, they pretended to be like *Fantomas*, master spy, disguiser-*par-excellence*, and soon we disappeared.

Our parents started leaving the country, families gone by morning, some to Spain, others to the United States, many never to come back. The neighborhood grew quiet. Houses emptied and new families moved in. Government people, my parents called them.

At night I dreamt of *Fantomas'* white car, pulling up to the front of the house, me and my parents getting in it, my father running his hands over the dials, the gadgets *Fantomas* would tell him not to touch. We'd drive away in a cloud of dust, down the street. We waved at our neighbors.

The white car drove to the edge of the water, over the sand, and kept going underwater. I could see coral reefs, schools of silverfish all around, and I would close my eyes to this intense opaline of water.

Who could wake up from this memory of vanishing?

Hilario, *El carretero del barrio*, Arroyo Naranjo, Cuba, circa 1969

He rang a bell he rigged by the wooden slat of his cart, where the cracks came together with wire and rusty nails. Twice he rang it, then his voice boomed down the street: *"Maní tostado, Maní. Se afilan cuchillos, tijeras, hachas."* He sold roasted peanuts. He also sharpened scissors, knives, axes. *"Pan dulce, pan dulce y caliente."* Sweet, hot bread.

The boys in the neighborhood snuck up and rode on the back of his cart as he made his way up and down the street, around the corner. Hilario knew we were back there, dangling our legs from the back, giggling. It was fine with him as long as we didn't steal a *cucurucho de maní*, a paper cone of peanuts, or a piece of his bread. The bread looked like the arms of angels under these pieces of wax paper he held down with clothespins and rocks so that the wind wouldn't blow them off.

We bought the bread when our parents gave us money: such sticky, sweet, caramel-scented bread, which we ate with great gusto in the shade of the plantain trees by the sidewalk. When he sharpened knives and scissors, orange sparks kicked up over his arms and his face. Each time he'd stop, lick his finger, then run it over the edge to check for sharpness. His fingertips were maps of cut skin, never healing, growing into calluses.

Our fathers said he was the best machete sharpener anywhere, leaving a shiny sliver of sharp edges.

Our parents felt sorry for Hilario and his cart, the way he

had to make a living, so they gave us money to buy from him. He was a skinny man with very dark, burnt-sugar skin. His deep-set eyes never looked at you straight. He was either drunk or there was something wrong with the way he looked up at people is what we always heard.

There was his missing leg, which, no matter how bad we treated him, we never dared bring up. We learned early never to mention his stump because it could literally cost us a couple of teeth. We were all afraid that Hilario would, in one swift swoop, cut off one of our ears with the sharpened dagger he kept tucked between his rope belt and his tattered pants.

On his arms were these faded, green-inked numbers everyone knew were his prison numbers from the years he'd spent at La Cabaña, Cuba's worst prison for political prisoners. Our parents said Hilario had spent twenty years there, starting with the Machado regime, then Batista, and even with Fidel. Everything that could be wrong with a person was wrong with Hilario. He stuttered and gasped as he tried to speak. He was missing his right leg, and whenever he climbed down from the cart to sharpen the knives, scissors, or shovels we brought him, his pant leg came loose and dangled there like the trunk of an elephant. Two of his fingers were missing, the stumps moving as he worked his hands. He chain-smoked, so his fingers were dirty yellow, half moons of grime and grease under his long nails.

When we made fun of him, called him *"El cojo,"* he told us to go fuck our own mothers. We loved to hear him say it, so we called him names all the time. And when we got him riled up, he'd start coughing and have to stop to catch his breath.

"Cabrones," he'd shout back at us. *"¡Algún día se van a acordar de mí!"* Someday you'll remember me. Once he told us the story of how he'd been a trainer of fighting cocks in Las Villas, where his own father gambled at the fights. He said he loved the way a rooster's feathers caught the light, held its iri-

descence for one brief moment, like a flash of silver and gold.

He dreamt of one day owning the best fighting cocks in the land. He knew how to train them well. His voice shook with conviction, and so we believed him for as long as we got to ride on his cart. We usually snuck up on him to ride on the cart. The cart was pulled by an old, mangy mule that kept shitting all over the place, including on its own hind legs. Nobody knew Hilario's real story, not us, not our parents, and Hilario never told us anything about himself, other than the stories of the cockfights.

When we angered him because he thought we didn't care about his roosters, he'd scream at us that we were all sissies, not knowing the difference between a rooster and a fighting cock. "*Un gallo campeón*," he said. Then he called us "*gallinas.*" Nothing but a bunch of hens, that's what we were to him. He knew to ignore us. He rode up and down the streets of the old neighborhood, shouting out the same things. If we caught up to him down the road we took to come back from school, we asked him for a ride, and he'd give us one as long as we went inside our houses and brought out money to buy his peanuts and bread. His cart creaked and rocked and got us there.

For years Hilario came through, and we came to depend on his stops, on his raspy voice calling out "*¡Pan dulce caliente! ¡Maní tostado!*"

Once we even saw the stump of his missing leg, right at the knee where the doughy-looking flesh folded and knotted into itself. Sometimes, he rubbed the air where the leg used to be. The day we saw it, he'd been wearing cut-off pant shorts. His good leg was skinny and full of scars as though someone had taken a machete and tried to hack him down. Sometimes we brought him cigarette butts and half-smoked cigars we found on the street because he'd trade peanuts for them so he could shred the tobacco and roll himself new smokes.

Nobody really knew where he lived, though some said he

came to Arroyo Naranjo from Calabazar, where everyone knew him, too. He traveled as far as the airport in Rancho Boyeros, where he loved to stop and watch the Russian and Cubana Airline's planes take off and land. He promised us once to take us there with him to watch. Then one day he stopped coming through, and for days we missed him, looked for him up and down our streets, around the corners, and no cart in sight, no trail of mule dung. Hilario disappeared from our neighborhood.

Our parents didn't know what had happened to him. Rumors set in. He'd been arrested for trafficking in black-market goods. He'd been accused by the CDR for counterrevolutionary activities. He'd hung himself from the branch of a ceiba tree. He'd been taken to Masorra for going crazy. He'd left the country clandestinely on a boat. On a raft. None of us knew what to believe, but our days were never the same. Nobody else came through to sell us the sweet bread, or the salted, roasted peanuts of our childhood.

We walked the dusty streets of our neighborhood, turning to the wind in hopes we'd catch his voice, or the clip-clop of his mule. Our own shadows began to catch up to us and scare us. These were beginning absences in our own lives, reminders of how long we still had to go. These began with Hilario, his mule and cart, his gnarled hands, his foggy, distant eyes, the way his empty pant leg moved in the wind, like a broken and tattered flag of our complete and unequivocal surrender in our childhood.

The Delgados's Son

The three times my parents visited, they took me with them to visit the family of Carlos Delgado, my father's friend from the Hatuey Brewery, where they worked the bottle-checking lines.

My father said that Carlos had never cut his hair, some kind of promise he'd made a long time ago. He and his family were devotees of San Lázaro, one of Cuba's major saints.

When you walked into the Delgado's home, you were greeted by a life-sized statue of San Lázaro, the leper, with replicas of the dogs licking his festering wounds around the old man's legs. The crutches were real wood crutches, armpit pads and all, and the old man's eyes followed you as you entered. The dog's, too. At least the one dog that was not licking. The statue stood on a small circumference of cement inside a large pond, where Carlos kept goldfish. The fish came up in a flash of orange and ivory, gulped down air, and dove to the black depth of the pond. Ferns grew all around the periphery of the pond, feather smooth, fleckled with seeds the size of pinheads underneath each leaf. The pond I liked—the statue and the dogs I found creepy. The three times we visited, I only tried to look at the fish, not at the old man looking down at me.

My parents insisted that I accompany them whenever they visited because they said the Delgados liked me. Mrs. Delgado always fed me these squared pieces of *melcocha,* a candy made out of pure brown sugar, or *boniatillo,* made from sweet yams. Also, my favorite, *raspacoco* made with coconut, hard on the teeth, extra sweet on the tongue. The first time I went, Bertha, as Mrs. Delgado liked to be called, spelled with the English h, took me to the kitchen, where I saw their altar to Santa Barbara, another Afro-Cuban deity.

On the altar there were candles, food, necklaces, red goblets full of *centavos*, Cuban pennies. She saw me looking and asked me, "*¿Es linda, verdad?*" Isn't she pretty?

I nodded my head yes, though again I couldn't bring myself to look at the Virgin's sad, porcelain-glossy eyes. They kept following me. Bertha was a short woman, with black hair and thick legs. She wore an amulet around her right ankle. It was made from red and black beads the size of coffee beans. What I liked about Mrs. Delgado, other than her sweet, delicious candies, were her hands. She had these small, perfectly manicured hands, ivory moons polished on each fingernail. I looked at them each time she gave me something to eat. She made lemonade, too. They had a lemon tree in their backyard.

After our first visit, I pretended to fall asleep in my father's arms as he and my mother walked back home from Carlos's and Bertha's house. I heard my mother kid my father about his liking Bertha. I almost said I liked her, too, but then I remembered I was pretending to be asleep because, although I was almost eight, I loved to be carried in my father's arms.

That first time we visited the Delgados and I was in the kitchen waiting for Bertha to reach to the cabinet and hand me the surprise treat, I heard a scratching on the door. I noticed Bertha stop in mid-opening of the cabinet door, and she looked at me and smiled. I thought it was the sound a cat makes trying to get inside the kitchen. Then the scratching stopped, and I thought I heard a hum.

That's when Bertha started asking me questions in a fairly loud tone. I thought she merely wanted for my parents to hear us in the kitchen. I don't know exactly why I thought that, but I did right there, standing close enough to her to smell the aroma of her perfume.

"How's school?" she asked.

I said, "Fine."

"You have friends?"

"A couple," I answered.

"What do you learn, at school?"

"History. Science. Math."

"Are you learning about Che and Camilo?"

Che and Camilo were revolutionary heroes in 1969, our last year in Cuba, the year we visited the Delgados three times. "Yes," I said, "and Fidel, too."

"*¿Y qué más?*" she asked, handing me a couple of treats.

I held one in my hands, and the other automatically went to my mouth. Soft *melcocha*, so sweet it made the words stick to the back of my throat, the walls of my mouth.

Suddenly, she took me out of the kitchen, and we returned to the living room where my parents sat with Carlos. They were drinking rum. I could smell it on my father's breath. My mother didn't like for my father to drink too much because he'd start talking about the island's situation, *la situación del país*, and about his wanting to get out, to leave. The walls have ears is what my grandmother always said, and my mother liked to tell that to my father.

"Carlos and I are good buddies. Right, Carlos?" my father would say.

"*Claro que sí, compay,*" Carlos would say and smile, then take a sip from his watermelon-print glass.

I was chewing on the delicious *melcocha*, listening to my parents talk with the Delgados. I kept looking all around at their heavy, brown furniture; the big, glossy floor tiles; the sound of the fish coming up for gulps of air kept coming from the pond; the miniature soldiers Carlos collected in a line behind a glass cabinet. I loved those soldiers. They were Roman gladiators, Royal Chinese Guards, Egyptians next to the scaled-down Sphinx, and Napoleon's armies at Waterloo.

Carlos always promised to open the cabinet and show them to me up close, but each time he'd try to do it, Bertha would pull him away. I would stay there looking at realistic *maquetas,* as Carlos called these battle scenes he made and painted.

In another cabinet he put together airplane models. He told my father that putting them together eased the tension in his hands, kept his mind off other things, if he knew what Carlos meant. My father would laugh at this and remind his friend he wasn't a surgeon. Both men would laugh as though they were already drunk.

"*No soy cirujano,*" Carlos would say and tremble with laughter so much his glasses would slide down the bridge of his nose, and his hair would fall in front of his eyes, the way it did when he sat behind the light checking defects in Hatuey beer bottles.

If it weren't for the fact that I loved to look at the soldiers and the model planes, I would have asked my parents to leave me at home with my grandmother, who read to me from the *Arabian Nights.* My favorite story out of that book was "Ali Baba and the Forty Thieves." I liked the way my grandmother pronounced, "*¡Ábrete Sésamo!*"

During our second visit, Carlos almost opened the cabinet where he kept his miniature soldiers. I almost got to touch one, when Bertha pulled him away to the kitchen. For the first time I realized that perhaps I'd never hold one of those little figures (and to this day I still wonder if my parents knew what was going on) when they kept doing that: Bertha taking Carlos to the kitchen, asking my parents for *disculpa.* "*Discúlpanos,* Suárez," that's what Bertha would tell my parents, and then they'd both disappear to the kitchen.

Of course, each time this happened, Bertha would return with tall, iced glasses of lemonade and more candies, cookies, little *pastelitos* she said she'd learned to make from her mother's recipe, her mother, bless her soul. *Guayaba* or mango pastries.

It was during that second visit, while Bertha and Carlos were in the kitchen and my parents were sitting in the living room, that I came very close to turning the cabinet's key and touching one of the soldiers, this Roman lashing four horses, two white and two black, pulling a golden chariot. The horses in the front had their front hooves lifted, giving them a fiery, bestial expression.

I was almost there when the screaming started. It sounded like the shrieking of a parrot or some animal coming from the kitchen. I turned the key to lock the cabinet and returned to my parents' side. They sat there as though they hadn't heard what I'd heard, my father sipping his lemonade, my mother looking at a *Bohemia* magazine.

I wanted to ask them if they had heard what I had. But I felt guilty for having almost opened the cabinet.

The screaming grew louder, a door opened, slammed shut. More screaming, then I heard Carlos pleading with someone in another room. Clearly, he said "no" three times. The last "no!" really resounded in the living room, and then everything returned to the usual silence.

My father sipped his lemonade.

My mother turned another page.

Bertha came back into the living room and joined my mother on the sofa. "Anything good?" she asked my mother.

My mother shook her head no.

Soon Carlos returned, too, his hair brushed back. He sat down with my father, and they started talking about the old days, when they both rode around on horseback, when they went fishing and hunting in Ciénega de Zapata. The turtles, the fish they caught, the cayman they killed.

On the way home that night, I walked between my parents.

There was a citywide blackout to save energy. At least that's the way our teacher explained it to us at school. In times of scarcity, the whole island needed to save energy. Who knew when the *yanquis* . . . that's what they called *Los Americanos*, people from the United States . . . *Los yanquis imperialistas*. The water would go out, too, which used to infuriate my grandmother. The only times I heard her curse were when the water got turned off.

"What happened?" I asked my parents as we all walked in the moonlight. There was a gentle breeze blowing in from shore. I heard it in the trees.

"Where?" my mother asked.

I asked about what had happened earlier. *Los gritos*, I said. The screaming.

My mother turned to my father and looked at him. Then they both looked down at me.

"The screaming?"

Come on, I thought, *surely you guys must have heard it, too*.

"Do they have a parrot?" I asked.

"No parrots," my father said.

"A dog?"

"No dog."

"A cat?"

"No cat."

During the third and final visit, I sat next to my mother on the sofa so that when the screaming started again, I'd nudge her on the side or pull on her skirt to let her know to listen.

After we entered and walked beyond the deep-set, following eyes of San Lázaro and his spooky, mangy dogs, we sat down in the living room. Carlos and Bertha, dressed up in pressed clothes, stood there by their furniture as though they had come back from a party or some place in Old Havana

where they'd gone to dance or to the movies. They looked very
made up.

They and my parents always talked about the American
movies, their favorite movie stars of the fifties and sixties. My
father always brought up John Wayne, my mother her favorite
of all time, Robert Mitchum in *Cape Fear*. Bertha adored Victor Mature, and Carlos always said he liked the comedians like
Charlie Chaplin, *El flaco y el gordo* (Laurel and Hardy), and
Jimmy Durante. He made fun of Jimmy Durante's nose. But
nobody could compare to Humphrey Bogart in *Casablanca* or
The Maltese Falcon. "*Ese americano es un bárbaro*."

I was waiting for a lull in the conversation to lure Carlos
back to the miniature cabinet, when the ruckus began in the
back room. Both Carlos and Bertha got up at the same time and
ran to the kitchen. There must have been a back room somewhere, someone kicking at the door, pounding with both fists
on wood, kicking and screaming.

"That noise," I said to my parents. "You hear it now?"

They both sat there quietly, turning their ears the way dogs
do when they hear a strange sound.

"Sure," my father said.

"I hear it, too," said my mother and sat up on the sofa.

Suddenly a door whipped open, and a naked, pink-fleshed
boy ran out toward us. His skin glowed, I swore. A red birthmark splotched on his back, the size of a sparrow. Purplish-red
toward the edges.

My father stood up as though the boy wasn't a boy but a
bull charging at him. The boy, tongue sticking out of his
mouth, long-haired, naked from head to foot, jumped on the
sofa next to my mother, rubbed himself against her, grabbed
her head and kissed her.

My father and I sat there stunned.

The bug-eyed boy had a hard and erect penis. Thin and
arched like a dog's. He held it and rubbed it, stuck a finger in

his mouth.

It's hard to say how much time passed between the boy's explosive attack on my mother and Carlos's running around after the boy whom he finally tackled on the floor. Carlos wrapped the boy's arms around so he couldn't move, lifted him up, naked and pink, into his arms, and ran him out of the room.

Bertha stood back right below the frame of the kitchen door, below the replica of "*Última Cena de Jesús Cristo*" and his twelve disciples. Crying, she held herself steady as her husband stormed past her.

Carlos's hair came undone, and he looked like a beast himself as he carried the boy out of sight. Then more screaming and banging. A door slamming shut, locking. A silence so deep we stood there shaking in its wake.

My mother and father stood up to go. I followed them to the door. My father stopped by the front door, right there by San Lázaro, his dogs, the goldfish coming up for air. I don't know what they were expecting. Maybe Carlos and Bertha to appear and say how sorry they were. *La disculpa.*

I turned to look at the statue's eyes following us out the door.

We closed the door behind us, and I never saw the Delgados again. On the way home my father told my mother that everyone in Cuba, everyone he knew, had secrets, but nothing like this.

I walked a little behind them. The moon was still full. The stars blinked and shone, cloistered in corners of the dark sky. It was a hot night. I kept replaying the scene, the boy storming into the living room, not wanting to believe it, the soldiers in the cabinet keeling over from the vibrations on the wood floor. The birthmark on his back opening like the wings of a bird. His erect penis like a flower in his hands.

For days and nights I daydreamed and had nightmares about what must have spooked that Roman soldier's chariot horses, the black ones rearing back on their legs, neighing at the precipice, at something unknown that held them back in this life.

Like the Delgados's son still screaming from that locked, back room of their house in Old Havana.

Initiation

Being an only son and growing up in Arroyo Naranjo, Cuba, in the late 1960s, I had never heard of *Los Corsarios Negros*. I found out about them via my schoolmates. *Los Corsarios Negros* was a gang on our street that hung out at the corner long after we young ones were in bed, under the billowed mosquito netting. I could hear them at the corner, their chatting like the sound of cicadas during the day, right before it rained.

It was a scary time in Cuba. People were leaving. Some disappeared. At school sometimes I'd show up and there'd be three new empty desks. The teachers would ignore the emptiness of those seats. Nobody wanted to say anything against the Revolution. Nobody wanted to speak out, but you could see the fear and concern in their eyes.

Certainly nobody wanted to talk about the police. Nobody wanted to mention the gangs like *Los Corsarios Negros*. But they existed, roaming free through the different neighborhoods, clashing with the police. Sometimes in the middle of the night we were awakened by loud reports of guns going off in the distance.

Sometimes I heard them break glass bottles, or pop tiny bombs that I learned to make later out of two screws and a thick nut, inside were as many matchheads as I could grind—and they'd be tossed up into the air and land with a pop. *Pop*. Sometimes the pop was loud enough to startle my grandmother in the other room, and she would tell my father, who would then step out onto the porch and shout at the boys on the corner.

Nobody really knew who belonged to the gang, but I heard rumors at school.

Fermín—the black kid who sat behind me in class and who also ate my pencil erasers as fast as the teacher gave them to me—told me that half of the class was in the gang. I looked around at all the other kids, dressed like me in their blue shirts, red kerchiefs around their necks, their hair combed neatly, cut short, like mine, scalloped at the front. No, I couldn't, or rather, wouldn't believe it. If some of these fools, I thought, could be in the gang, so could I.

At home I told my best friend Ricardito, who lived at the corner of the block, right next to us, but he was too afraid. Lanky and tall, he was a bit awkward, uncoordinated. When we rode bikes, he fell; if we skated, he always skinned his elbows and knees—no, he'd have no part of it. On the playground one day, I approached three boys, all taller and bigger than me, and I simply asked what it took to be a part of the gang, the infamous *Corsarios*. I thought they were pirates because my grandmother had read me stories of pirates in the port of New Orleans, always making the stories sound exotic, far, far away. I loved those stories.

The Black Corsairs roamed the Havana nights pulling pranks, breaking windows, deflating car tires, setting trash cans on fire, stealing the fruit from our trees. Their mischief was endless. The three boys eyed me as though I had asked them something in Greek or Chinese. They looked beyond me at the teachers keeping vigil on the playground. I remember the day, one of those radiant Havana days, not a cloud in the sky, a warm breeze making the almond tree leaves flicker and reflect the sunlight, like hands waving. The boys took me aside and asked me where I had heard of the gang. They told me I could only join if I promised not to ever utter the name of the gang, which I did immediately in my head: *Los Corsarios Negros. Shhh. Shhh.*

They told me to meet them that night at the corner of Balmaseda and Luz, that I had to sneak out and meet them there at the corner. All day I kept planning how I would sneak out of the house. My parents always listened to music on the radio late into the evening, after dinner, with my grandmother talking about the old days. I couldn't leave through the front door. My mother always locked the back door and then stacked a whole bunch of pots and pans—her own *alarma*, she called it, meaning if someone opened the door there'd be a ruckus so loud it would wake us all up, and then?

I thought of another way of getting out of the house. I knew how to remove the glass panes of the window in my room. They had a latch, and I could remove the panes one by one; all I needed to do was to remove four of them. At seven, I was a small, skinny kid—one of my uncles called me *El Majá*, which I learned later was a joke in reference to Goya's "La Maja." But *El Majá* meant a kind of Cuban snake, very common in our back yards.

I once killed a brown one by the rabbit cages with my father's machete. It rose up as if to bite me, and I swung and chopped its head clean off. The rest of it I watched wiggle and form these small and big Ss. This was the same snake who was rumored to have eaten babies in the neighborhood. Once, the story goes, a sugarcane cutter fell asleep under the shade of a guayaba tree, and the snake ate up his leg while he slept. Another man had to cut open the snake to free the man's leg.

I thought of slithering, wriggling like a snake. I liked snakes, even though I knew to keep my distance. So that's what I would do, I thought. I would remove the windowpanes, and jump out the window. Then I thought of the chickens my father kept corralled on that side of the house. What if I startled them in their sleep and they started to cackle? I would slither out, I told myself. After all, I was *El Majá*, about to join *Los Corsarios Negros*.

That night, with a great deal of anticipation, I ate all my food, washed up, and told my parents I was going to bed—even my grandmother looked at me and then asked if I felt okay. I simply told them what I had rehearsed: I was very tired. It had been a long day at school, which was partly true because they had made us march in unison around the flagpole, stop, sing the national anthem, march more, stop, sing, march, stop, sing, march. We were going to be taken on a field trip to Plaza de la Revolución in Havana, where El Máximo Líder was going to give a speech, like those I had stayed up with my parents to hear (and falling asleep throughout) in front of the television, which only seemed to work when there were rallies and speeches.

While my parents cleaned up the table and then came to the living room to chat, I removed the glass panes of the window very slowly. One by one. I kept checking on the chickens right outside the window. I kept going *ssh-ssh*, just to get them used to the small noises and sounds I would be making, if I had to make any noise at all. With the third slat removed, I knew I could sneak out. The fourth one I placed on my mattress and then placed my pillow on top of it. I clambered out and, sure enough, some of the chickens got startled but they didn't make a sound.

I climbed on top of the henhouse, then onto the cement fence right by Ricardito's bedroom window. From there I'd climb onto the roof, as I had done during the days when I went up on the roof to play, to pretend I was a pilot in the air force, knocking down the yellowed coconuts from the palm trees in our front yard. I was like a cat, not just a snake; already I felt proud that I was almost going to be a *Corsario*.

Once on top of the roof, I went around toward the corner, making sure not to catch one of my shoelaces on a roof tile and fall. I didn't want Manuel or Josefina waking up, if they were

sleeping. Like my parents, they were probably listening to the
radio, too. They didn't have a television, and that's how
Ricardito and I became such good friends. He was always over
to watch the cartoons, like Porky Pig and Mighty Mouse.

Once at the corner, I jumped onto a tall papaya tree and slid
down, scraping my forearms a little, but I didn't care. I was
ready for more.

The corner was really dark, because the boys had already
knocked out the lights. I didn't hear anything at all. The whole
street was dark, and I could see a couple of *cucuyos*, fireflies,
flickering across the street by the corner trash dump. I waited,
and nothing. I started to bite my fingernails, feeling nervous
and excited.

I waited what felt like all night, and nobody came. I
watched my own shadow and then I started to get afraid. Just
when I was about to leave, I heard the sound of a car speeding
down the street. A black car drove past me, turned at the corner, and then stopped in front of my house. I heard its door
open. I walked closer and saw two men getting out of the car.

What kind of trouble was I in? I couldn't help but imagine.
I hurried around the back, jumped over two fences. I couldn't
climb on the roof again, but I came in through the back of our
house, jumped a smaller chain-link fence, and just as I was
climbing back into my room, I heard a knock on the door.

One heave and I climbed up onto the windowsill, my
elbows scraping on the wall. I felt the rough edges cut my skin.
I could see my grandmother turn off the radio, and once I was
back in my room, I heard my mother whisper something or
other to my father. I heard her say the men were G-2. *G-2?*
Special police agents. Secret police.

They wanted to speak with my father at the station. I heard
my father go to the door.

Before I was born, he had been a policeman, and rumor
had it, he still had his gun. In all the hours I spent snooping

around in drawers and behind the furniture, I never found it, but I heard two of my uncles who visited us talking about it. My parents wanted to leave the country. My father had already announced it to my mother's huge family. Very few people were happy about it, but my father said he mostly worried about my future, how they needed to get me out of Cuba before I was drafted into the army.

"What do you want?" I heard him ask them.

"Come with us," they said.

I stepped onto the bed, having forgotten the pane of glass on the mattress, and I broke it. I heard it snap like a bone under my foot. I jumped down in time to hear one of the men tell my father he had to accompany them. I heard my mother's voice crack with concern.

"*Se llevan a Villo, Isabel*," she told my grandmother

My grandmother told my mother to go with my father.

They took my mother, too.

My grandmother locked the door behind them, and then I heard her in the kitchen. She opened the faucet, but there was no sound of water. I came out of the room.

I heard her saying, "*No lo puedo creer. No lo puedo creer.*" She couldn't believe it.

She saw that I was dressed, also noticed my bleeding elbows and forearms.

"*¿Qué te pasó, niño?*"she asked me.

I wanted to know what was going on with my father.

She asked me what I was doing dressed.

She took a dishrag and wet it, brought it over and cleaned the blood off my elbows, my arms, my fingers.

I was not going anywhere.

I asked about my parents. Where did they go?

Not to worry, my grandmother told me, and said that they'd be right back.

She came to my bedroom and helped me take off my

clothes, to get back in bed. When she turned down the sheet, she saw the broken glass. I explained it to her. She didn't understand, but she had more on her mind.

The gaping hole in my window she could deal with later, but my parents' absence made her shake. She changed the sheet where there were pieces of glass, then put me to bed. She kept me company long after both of our hearts had quieted.

The house was dark.

I heard the chickens flinch on their perches.

No other sounds.

The mosquito netting hung above us, enveloped us like an open mouth.

Then I asked my grandmother, who was holding my hand tight, to tell me another story about *Los Corsarios Negros* of New Orleans.

Blown

You come to the Toucan Club on Sunset Boulevard to sober up.

This is the best place in Los Angeles where you can sit and relax and listen to Latin jazz. Your favorite hangout. Something about the lights swirling, these blurs and flashes against the smooth, shiny surfaces. A constant clink of glasses, voices talking, laughter, good times, what the living must do.

The girl you are with, Carla, wants to go some place else, but you're too tired and strung out to keep partying. Not much conversation between you two, but she keeps asking for the little plastic bag and running to the bathroom to do a couple more lines.

Her nervousness is annoying. Or is it her greed? She blows coke like she does everything else, with complete abandon. Maybe it bothers you because you hate to be alone. It's when you find yourself alone that you start to think about all the things you don't want to think about, like war, bad marriages, children who no longer speak to their fathers. You used to be an asshole, but living into your forties mellows everyone out.

※↑↑↑

The band, five guys in tropical carnival-type outfits, comes back from a break and picks up their instruments. Some of their songs are new, which makes you wonder how long it has been since the last time you were here. The waitress keeps returning to your table to clean the ashtray, and replace the hot sauce or corn chips. Each time she makes conversation, which

43

is something you appreciate. Her hair is tied into a ponytail, a turquoise band holding it back. Very nice. She tells you the place is hopping tonight. She likes it when it is this crowded. A crowd means more tips, more conversation. More electricity. She's been bringing you stiff drinks, double alcohol. You think she likes you. For these reasons, you think, you'll leave her a Benjamin Franklin.

Carla walks back to the table quickly, trying not to stagger. Braless, her small round breasts bounce under the silk of her V-shaped, white dress, her nipples dark as pennies, erect. There's a birthmark on her right breast, you remember, which darkens when her nipples become aroused.

"Ordered you another White Russian," you say, reaching over and wiping her upper lip with your thumb. She's twenty-two, a college drop-out turned court stenographer. For someone who spends her days taking words down, she hardly talks.

"Can't handle it," she says, handing you the bag under the table.

"Drink coffee."

"Coffee and coke don't mix," she says, then puts her house keys into her leather purse.

"Sure they do."

"Coke and holy water don't."

"You mean 'fire' water." *Aguardiente*. Rotgut stuff.

You check the Ziplock with your finger to make sure that the bag is sealed, then drop it into your shirt pocket without looking at the bag.

"Any left?" you say.

"Enough to get us home," she says and cuts a smile.

She lives like this most of her days. She lives in Glendale with two cats and a Chihuahua who keeps chewing the leather of your shoes, tucking them under the bed. At night you don't go to the bathroom because you don't want to step on it by accident, you don't want to hear the yawp-yawp and door scratching. Her mother is dead. Her father is dead. No brothers or sisters. She's as alone as you are.

But you like the way she looks, firm arms and thighs, strong abdomen, her short hair. The way she pronounces each word as though she's got something sweet in her mouth. Like now when she says "home."

The way she pronounces "home" makes you think of what the two of you will do there. More liquor, of course. And coke, to speed things up. In the bedroom you'll watch her undress, slip off the G-string undies slowly, knowing you are watching. The smooth skin of her back.

The waitress brings the drinks and sets them away from your hands. She's still smiling. You take a sip of your Remy Martin and hold it in your mouth for a while, then swallow it quickly. The waitress wipes the ashtray clean, picks up her tray, and leaves. "Let's toast to life," you say, raising your glass.

"Fuck life," Carla says. "Keep inventing stories."

This is what she calls you opening up, revealing a few things about your life, like the times you lived in Cuba. How you got out.

"Toast to that," you say.

"And to whatever's left in your pocket."

This is what you see when you look at the mirrored wall behind Carla: a pale face, a receding hairline, your hair swept back by the wind from driving your convertible Spitfire, and narrow eyes too distant for you to see how utterly bloodshot they are.

"I bet you didn't know I was in Vietnam," you say.

"A Cuban in Vietnam?"

You notice how her fingers shake as she takes a cigarette out of the YSL Ritz pack.

"When the time came, everybody went," you say.

"Not everybody."

"You were here?" you ask.

"Cuba," she says and looks at the man playing the electric piano. He jumps up and down as he starts his solo.

"Like I said, I went."

"All right," she says. "How many did you kill?"

"I got there at the end. Before I knew it, I was back."

"That's anticlimactic."

"So what."

"You saw no action over there?"

"You know, the usual. Helicopters airlifting the wounded. Huts firebombed to ashes. Some bombing."

"And nothing happened to you?"

"Not a scratch," you say. You take a cigarette and light it.

"I can't believe it."

You can smell what people are drinking, smoking around you. So much perfume, enough to make you feel light-headed.

"Documentary footage stuff. That's it." You blow smoke into her face.

There is a moment of silence between songs when you have to lower your voice.

"I don't like the way you make it sound," Carla says. The way she stares at your fingers makes you wish you knew what she is thinking about.

"I'll spare you the details."

She crushes the cigarette on the ashtray, then finishes whatever is left of her drink.

You continue: "See, I attend these group sessions at the VA hospital. The government pays for it, so I go."

"In other words," she says, "you're abusing—"

"Let me finish," you say, "they think I'm fucked in the head like most of these other guys in there."

"There's nothing wrong with you," she says, then begins to laugh.

"I love going to the meetings. That's how I find out what I missed. Some of these guys tell great stories. Sometimes they piss me off because they don't want to believe I was there."

"I believe you."

"Something funny happened during one of the meetings. I can't remember what I was trying to say, but I got so frustrated I stood up and clapped my hands." You clap your hands loud enough to startle the couple sitting at the next table. They look at both of you briefly, then return to their business.

"All the patients hit the floor," you say, "but I'm the only son of a bitch standing. Except for the counselor. There they were, cupping their hands over their ears."

"That was funny?" she asks.

"I'm going to keep doing it for the hell of it—"

"You still attend?"

"If I ever get caught for dealing," you say, "I can plead insanity. Blame it on the war."

"They know you sell drugs for a living?"

"Sure, but they don't care. Those guys have tried everything. Even suicide."

Carla fidgets with her purse, looks for something within it, but doesn't find it.

"Everybody in there's fucked up."

The waitress comes over to find out if you want anything else. You tell her you're fine for now, but that in a while you might need another round.

"Speaking of another round," Carla says, looking at your shirt pocket.

"Not hooked?" you say.

"We can go to the beach later," she says.

"When we wake up." You take a drag of your cigarette.

"I've got nothing to do tomorrow," she says.

"Correction, today."

"We've got nothing to do today."

"Bacardi awaits at home," you say, fishing for the plastic bag in your pocket.

"I promise, I won't do it all," she says.

You give her the bag. She takes it to the bathroom again, where she stays for a long time. You wonder if she's sharing it with some of the other women in the stalls.

Alone again, you watch how the band keeps the rhythm up by dancing while they play their instruments. Glitter sparks off their billowing shirt sleeves. The couples around you have left their tables for the dance floor.

Carla is all you can think about.

You imagine her inside one of the bathroom stalls, leaning over the toilet, scooping out a tiny mound of the white powder with one of her little flattened spoons or a house key, and snorting it.

Or she might be simply going to the bathroom, looking at the floor cracks. Like little rivers, you think.

You signal the waitress. She comes over and you order another round. Before she leaves, you drop the one-hundred-dollar bill on her tray and thank her. She looks surprised. For the steady, well-done supplies. Toast to that, she says. A little something to make her night.

She leans close to your ear and says thank you. Her breath smells of peppermint. A faint aroma of papaya shampoo in her hair. Her warm hand on your shoulder, a gentle squeeze.

You watch her dance her way back to the bar.

Nights like this are meant for everything broken—things, people, shards of light across the floor like skin. Your job is to pick them up, dead fingers, ears, one by one, string them around your neck, their sweet scent wafting to your nostrils. It's only a matter of time. This rushing of thoughts about people and places you want to forget. The damaged, hollowed left behind. Nights like this, the world should catch fire, burn to the ground, ravage the land in one giant swoop of flame, taking you with it, so you can move on.

Conduit

La conductora, the woman at number 51, the corner house with the red door, she with curlers in her hair. Every day she sends the neighborhood kids out to steal eggs, chickens, broken-down furniture for her stove, on which she cooks tamales, which her husband sells on foot.

She is better known as the woman other neighbors come to see about this business of electricity. See, she's the one with the power lines coming across the street, from the main lines, to a pole which she can reach from her kitchen window, and she runs her web of lines all through the neighborhood for a nominal fee. Of course, nobody can snitch on her because she happens to be the president of *El comité*, which controls mostly everything.

Between her power, her cooking, and her husband's sales, they live. She says, *así vamos viviendo*; you make due in this land of necessity, mother of invention. The house is falling apart brick by brick, panel by panel.

The children bring her lime, which she dilutes with water in buckets and fills-in holes, paints every month, especially during the stormy months, when downpours wash everything through the cobbled streets to the river, then out to sea. She can see this from her makeshift balcony as she dries clothes, cleans fish, and smokes meat.

It is from here she keeps her eyes open for any Yankee invasion.

At night, she says, she comes out to smoke her cigars and look out beyond the bay's buoys and beacons. She looks out for battleships, planes, anything suspicious, and every day she spots them, the people on rafts, leaving, waving good-bye.

She can't believe it: how often they go away, never to come back. She keeps her mouth shut because anybody crazy enough to get on an inner tube or a shambled raft deserves a chance at making it, or maybe not.

When they dip into the horizon, she closes her eyes and spits on the ground. The cigar embitters her saliva.

She utters a prayer under her breath, a litany of words that run out of her like the electricity she harvests—these currents coming in, coming through.

Grandmother's Instructions

If we flew, not to look at the clouds for too long—they spoke too much anger.

If we sailed, seawater could never show us the way. Stars would.

When upon free soil, bow to the four directions to pay the wind homage.

When asked for papers, show the fire in our hands, how charmed the flames play.

In traffic, take off our red shirts or skirts and scream, "Ah-ha! Toro! Olé!"

Beware of used furniture given to us; a worn sofa swallows not only money, but luck.

In times of plenty, serve an extra plate, always with rice.

In times of scarcity, think of our lives in the old country. Do not mistake "want" for "lack."

Never look into a mirror that reflects another mirror or else get lost in the infinity of place.

Always leave the front door open, a horseshoe nailed to the inside archway.

Speak of how much water the sky gave the earth, how seeds sought light after a dark spell.

In springtime open the windows of our new house, invite the birds to feed.

In the fall, leave a glass of water under the bed, watch for how dust gathers in corners.

At night when we close our eyes to sleep, think of her as a gardenia flower, an open hand waving good-bye atop her grave.

Corners

Raúl stands on the curb as his boss's green van turns the corner. Good riddance, Raúl thinks, what an asshole. Ortega, his father's friend who gave him this job for the summer, is a tightwad, and that van of his is a rolling disaster. Any morning now it's going to fall apart over the railroad tracks. Raúl can see those front wheels spinning off their drums, rolling down the street, and the van grinding its nose into asphalt, a beached green whale. This thought makes Raúl smile as he bends over and picks up the wire scraper, brushes, and the can of brick-red paint he needs to start on the day's work.

He hates this line of work. Actually, no, he hates all work. He'd much rather be playing ball at the park, but that already got him in trouble. Not only with his parents, sure, but with the police. The cops came to the park to harass him and his friends. Because, the cops said, someone complained about their loitering.

What's a park for? he asked the bodybuilding cop, knowing all along he was showing off in front of his friends. The cop didn't appreciate his smart-alecky ass, so he cuffed him and took him in, and because Raúl wouldn't shut up in the back when they arrived at the station and parked, the cop grabbed him by the hair and pulled him out of the back. It hurt like a mother.

Of course his parents got called in, and now, he's here practically working free for Ortega, the fat, greasy bastard.

"*¿Qué piensas tú?*" his father asked, driving back home from the police station. "Do you think this kind of behavior is okay?"

Raúl sat in the back seat and looked at the backs of his parents' heads, his mother nodding each time his father spoke. His father only spoke in questions. Questions for which Raúl had grown tired of predictable answers. "*La vida* is going to teach you some tough lessons," his mother told him.

Raúl stands there on the sidewalk by the dying walnut tree and looks at the apartment building in this part of Long Beach called Little Cambodia. He can't believe his rotten luck. Shit, shit, shit, he curses and moves closer.

The duplex, one of the many properties Ortega owns in Little Cambodia, is run-down, all the window woodwork rotting, making the facade look droopy, like in the cartoons. Stained, raggedy curtains hang behind the cracked glass. The grass grows back in clumps among the patches of weeds. The stucco cracks run like rivers up and down the sides. Sparrows have built bushy nests from every other roof-tile hole, which Ortega expects him to empty. Raúl can see it now—he'll be up there pulling those nests out, the eggs or chicks falling thirty feet to the ground.

First, Raúl must do all the prep work on the wood, mostly rotted, termite-infested, scrape, prime, and paint. It's a lot of fucking work, he thinks, three bucks an hour, bring your own lunch, one break. It's not fair, he wants to say, but his parents warned him if he didn't do this, off he went to Miami to live with his Nazi uncle who promised to shape Raúl up. His uncle owns a shipyard on the Miami River, and he often tells Raúl's father, his brother, to send Raúl down. Yeah, send the boy down, we'll put him to weld underwater. Sure. Who needs it.

The way Raúl sees it, he'll work this bullshit job all summer, then finish high school and then hit the road. Go where he wants to go. Hell, he might even go to college, if one takes him in. He'd like to play soccer somewhere, if someone is willing to give him a tryout. Hell, the way he sees it, he's only sixteen. It's only a matter of time before someone notices him. He wants to go far. Very far. Only he's stuck here for the time being. It's the waiting around he hates. The going nowhere. No use daydreaming if you've got to concentrate on painting and scraping, the stuff any fool can do.

Morning and already the sun breaks through, strong and hot. Raúl wipes the sweat off his brow and tips the visor of his baseball cap down to keep the glare out of his eyes. Ortega's due to swing by at noon to check up on him, make sure he's still at work. The shade under one of these eucalyptus trees by the side sure looks good. He could simply lie down and nap, but he doesn't want to get his parents riled up again. He's caught, he thinks, caught like a fucking tuna in a net. He's seen them on television.

During the week he's been working for Ortega, Raúl has become a good fix-it-all, handyman—that is, when he wants to, when he tries, when he gets going on thinking about the possibilities of where he'll go play ball. His mother, also under Ortega's employ at his clothing factory, demands that Raúl do a good job for Ortega, or else. It is the "else" Raúl likes to ponder.

His parents even grounded him for a month. No driving. No friends over. No soccer. This was serious fucking business, his parents said. His father called him a couple of cuss words in Spanish. Raúl still thinks about them: *comemierda, estupido*. He translates them into English: shit-eater, stupid. First time his father ever called him this, though he'd heard his father call other people that. What could he do? Raúl feels like things aren't going to work out for him. He fears getting stuck, stranded in the same life he sees his parents have. Work, work, work. Get up early. Go to work. Come home tired. Go to bed early because they have to go to work. "Bullshit," Raúl mutters.

Work is for losers. The only thing he wants to work hard at is his sport.

Little Cambodia is no different from where he comes from, Raúl thinks. Almost the same worn, tired look to everything. The trees. Buildings. Potted plants. The old folk coming and going. Why is it that the old get that curve on their backs? Who invented the undershirt old immigrant men wear? In this heat, amazing, he thinks. The women with their basset-hound sadness to their eyes. Those dark sunglasses that wrap around their heads and make them look like aliens.

The loud voices of kids playing in a vacant lot across the street rise behind him. Scattered trash clutters the lot. The kids use an old sofa as if it were a pirates' ship. Always, there are kids in the neighborhood. Except here it's the Vietnamese children.

Over in his neighborhood are Mexican kids, Nicaraguan kids, Cubans like him and his parents. There, Cuban old men play dominos and drink rum—at Christmas-time, they roast the pigs in old, cut-open oil drums. They make such a big deal about those pigs. His father's friends—Ortega is one—come over and talk loud, get pretty obnoxious, talking about the old country, life here in the United States, where everything is work, work, work.

Oh, and all the advice, somebody or other is always putting a hand on Raúl's shoulder to give him advice: on girlfriends, on school, on cars, on life. The best one comes from his own father: "Don't cut corners or you turn twice."

He doesn't get it, any of them, all this advice in Spanish. When he translates them into English, they don't make any sense. They become noise in his ears.

Behind the lot, endless clotheslines, from which multicolored clothes hang, blocking the view of the tenements. For a moment Raúl thinks he knows what kind of people live there. He has been here many times.

This is the way it probably looks in the old country. This clutter of life on the move. Getting nowhere. But he is, he thinks, he plans to get somewhere. Hopefully far.

According to Ortega, this neighborhood's made up of Cambodians, Mexicans, and Americans who refuse to move away. The Cambodians who live in the duplex are never late paying the rent.

While he scrapes the loose flakes, Cambodian children peek out of the front window by the side of the porch. The tallest one, his short hair cropped unevenly over his large, curious eyes, smiles at Raúl. A sort of peek-a-boo. At first it is funny, but then the kid keeps doing it, so it begins to grate on his mood. An hour later, the kid is still looking at him with his almond-colored eyes, his short spiky hair, his nose with the pinched nostrils, the birthmark splotched on his neck.

Raúl works away at removing the old paint, brushing as hard as he can to get it all off. Years, he thinks, it has been here, each time the new layer covering the old. And every time he looks up, the kid is there looking out at him paint. Raúl feels like painting the glass so the kid can't look at him anymore. Spooky little shit.

Raúl remembers in history class the teacher showing them a documentary about the Vietnam war. He remembers the scene with the naked girl running, behind her, black clouds of a fire-bombed village, and the soldier who shoots the man in the head, point-blank. He remembers the girls in the class going "turn it off, turn it off" and one of the guys saying "shit-out-of-luck."

Gross. Sickening. The teacher made them shut up and pay attention, himself a veteran now teaching them in Los Angeles, the "freshly arrived," as the teacher called them.

"We keep getting the world out of trouble," Mr. Salvatore said, "and the world expects it from us. Bad decisions made on our part. Vietnam costs us more than we are willing to pay again. Fifty thousand casualties. Many more lost every day to drugs. Madness. Suicide . . ."

Mr. Salvatore would get so upset sometimes that he'd have to walk outside the classroom and get some fresh air. Raúl would run to the bungalow window and check him out, make sure the coast was safe so that he could rewind the video and freeze it on the naked girl, the guys pointing to her crotch.

The paint, as Raúl brushes it in quick, even strokes, covers the stairs smoothly—no need for a second coat, he thinks. He sops it on thick. No way he's coming back another day to do this. If he could have it his way, he'd take off. Teach his parents a lesson. Maybe hit the road, leave for good.

When these feelings of being stuck invade him, Raúl cringes, bites down on his lip simply to control the rage welling up inside him. He fears not being able to stay in control.

Suddenly the front door opens, and the tall Cambodian kid appears.

"Me and my brothers go play," the kid says.

"Use the back door," Raúl says.

"Back door parents lock."

Fresh paint covers the steps between the kid and Raúl. The kid stands there, his knobby knees almost touching, his thin, long toes looking dirty and weird.

"You'll have to wait, okay?" Raúl says.

"You pick me up," the kid says.

"Can't reach you from here."

"I play now!"

The little monster, Raúl thinks, and says, "When the paint dries, okay?" Give him a break.

Raúl remembers Mr. Salvatore's talk about one culture dumping on another. It's the history of civilization. It's the history of the United States. The dominant culture taking advantage of the weak.

"I tell my grandmother," he says and closes the door.

A group of kids runs across the street screaming like Indians on the attack. Girls stand by the side fence, giggling, pointing to the group of boys on the torn sofa.

If he could only be at the park now, Raúl thinks, playing soccer with his friends. What am I doing here? he thinks.

Above him, the hungry sparrow chicks cry for their parents to bring them food, and each time Raúl looks up, he can't see them. He wishes he could, but that would mean he'd have to carry the ladder over and set it up. Their cries are constant. No parents in sight.

Almost like these kids. Where are the parents?

When he finishes the first handrail, he moves the paint and brushes to begin on the other.

The kids behind the fingerprint-smudged glass stick their tongues out at Raúl as he steps back for a look at what he has accomplished. Not even paint can help, he has decided, so why keep trying?

Raúl grins up at them.

The door opens again, and this time an old Cambodian woman with the wrinkles of a bedsheet fresh on her face stands there, arms akimbo.

"It's wet," Raúl tells her.

She looks down at the paint. Her pants come up halfway between her knees and her ankles. She, too, has ugly feet, her toes curving inward because of these great bunions. She's missing a toe on her left foot.

"Understand?" he says, dipping the paintbrush into the can. "It's wet. Wet."

The woman says something in Cambodian to the kid behind her.

"What you doing?" the kid asks.

"Tell her Ortega told me to paint the porch," Raúl says. "The boss man. The owner of the apartments."

The kid speaks to his grandmother, who then pushes her grandson back inside and closes the door.

One day he's going to make sure he doesn't own property, run-down shitholes like this one, Raúl thinks. He's not going to let big families live in the apartments he will never own. He can't see himself as the owner of anything. Well, maybe a car. His own house in which to live. Sure, that he can handle.

But no kids. Too many kids get out of hand; they ruin everything.

A few strokes short of finishing, the tall kid runs out of the apartment, stepping on the paint. His little footprints on the still-wet paint. Raúl cannot believe it. The kid has balls.

Raúl chases after the kid, catches up, and picks him up by the waist.

"Let go!" the kid says, banging on Raúl's back. "Let go, you!"

"Little bastard," Raúl yells. "Didn't I tell you to wait until the paint dries, huh?"

Raúl carries the kid back to the apartment, where the grandmother waits.

"Keep his ass inside," Raúl tells her. He tries to let her know with one look how angry he is. Can't they see he doesn't want to be here? He's not coming back to paint all this again, no way.

She yanks the kid back inside and shuts the door. The blackened doorknob rattles when she slams the door.

Ortega'll be here soon, Raúl thinks, trying to find a way to cover up the foot marks. This, he guesses, is the kind of shit he'll have to put up with for the rest of the summer. Here, in the other properties, everywhere he goes to paint.

When he talks to his friends at school, they make fun of him because he's trying too hard to fit in. He wants to blend, melt—whatever it is they call it in history class. This melting-pot big deal. How people come to the United States and take part in American daily life. How they enter the mainstream and begin to lose their old culture. Raúl doesn't care about that. He wants to be left alone to do what he likes to do. He has lived in this country longer than anywhere else. He doesn't even remember Cuba, where he was born. His parents sure do remember it, always talk to him about it. But he lives here now. This is where he's going to make it.

All the paint in the world couldn't begin to hide all the shit of the world. He straightens and laughs at his own thought. He imagines those brush-fire helicopters carrying, instead of buckets of water, buckets of paint, drizzling paint on every city in Los Angeles County, over everything, houses, trees, cars, people. People will come out of their houses to go to work or school and Splash! Get painted. Ruined dresses. New suits. Work clothes. And he'd paint everything an ugly, bright purple, or maybe blue. He likes the possibilities of blue. He can almost hear his father on the phone, complaining to the authorities that his son has gone crazy painting everything in the neighborhood blue.

Once he finishes covering up the marks, Raúl walks to the nearest tree and sits in the shade to wait for the van. Ortega will soon arrive to pick him up, take him to another place in need of paint.

How can he give up on his summer? Raúl thinks. This one summer in his sixteenth year. No way, man. But everything points in the direction of waste. Going up in the heat of this day.

Suddenly, the front door flings open. Raúl bolts up into a sitting position. He can't believe it.

The kid runs outside again—this time, his brothers and sisters follow. Their grandmother watches as they cross the street. A car almost hits the last one, who is completely naked.

Raúl stands, approaches the woman, and says, "Why did you let them out?"

The woman leans against the door frame with a look of satisfaction widening her gray eyes.

"Lady," he says, raising his voice, "I'm trying to get this job done." He's going to tell Ortega to evict their asses out of here, he wants to say, but doesn't say it. He holds the words in, and they choke him, they become bricks in his throat, hard and unpalatable.

All the paint's gone, so Raúl has to get water out of the faucet by the side of the house and thin some of the paint at the bottom of the can. No matter how many times he runs the brush over the stairs, the footprints remain. "The little son of a bitch," Raúl says under his breath. "I should kick his Cambodian ass."

Ortega's green van is due to turn at the corner any minute now.

Pushing the other kids off the sofa, the Cambodian kid jumps up and down, kicks up clouds of dust around their feet and legs. They are shouting something in Cambodian to Raúl. He knows they are mocking him, making fun of him for all the times he has fucked up. For all the times he has held back. For all his failures.

Raúl bends over the stairs and tries frantically to cover the marks. The oldest kid pounds on his chest like some great gorilla and howls at the top of his lungs. Raúl feels like none of this is part of what he came here to do. Suddenly, sadness fills him like this coat of thin paint he has laid down. Not enough color to cover the old, the worn, the utterly ugly. Like so much of his life, he thinks. He's beginning to think that around the corner, there's no way out. Nowhere to go. Dead ends everywhere.

The Cambodian children mock him. They point accusatory fingers at him as if to say: *you, you're not one of us, you don't belong here.*

Their howls are loud enough to get the sparrow chicks crying all over again.

Jinetera Currency

On the streets they call it *fula, guano, guaniquiqui*, all words that mean dollar. Cuban youth will do anything for some, like show you parts of their bodies, legs spread or buttocks, a mango in the mouth, at play with a green banana. Men come from all over the world to defile children, poison them with the sleeplessness of their own nights. *Jineteras calientes*, someone calls out in the dark streets of Old Havana, windows lit by candlelight: hot young women!

Here, they're in Lycra outfits, the contours of their bodies maraca smooth. If you shake them, spoiled fruit will fall from their armpits, their soiled youth. They come from as far as the islands of Santiago and Matanzas. At thirteen or fourteen, they are already violated by some men, sometimes strangers, sometimes not.

They've heard word of money in Havana, how easy it can be made, a nocturnal lingo for the exchange of flesh. The Italian men are the worst—then the Spanish, balding, drooling saliva froth on their nipples, loose ball sacks, gray-haired pubis.

When the morning comes, they rinse out their mouths with rum, a sting of anger on their lips, a raven meanness for carcass. Some think of plunging a hairpin into their tricks' hearts, but that would mean prison or death.

So they leave as soon as the bastards are done, clean up and go, back to the street where the salty warm breeze from off shore cools them back to their senses.

Only to begin again.

In this island of abrupt endings, nobody's keeping score.

Grease

Álvaro's garage stank of car fumes, or spilled gasoline, which made me dizzy ever since I was a kid in Cuba and one of my father's friends visited on his Indian motorcycle. I remember it well, how he kick-started it with a belch of blue-cloud smoke.

At Álvaro's garage all of my father's friends gathered in the late afternoon, after they all drove there from their factory jobs. I walked there from the high school on Miles Avenue. The garage stood at the corner of Sepúlveda and Gage, right across from a Winchel's Donut Shop, where, if I had some money left over from lunch, I'd buy a glazed donut or apple fritter. Most of the time, I simply stayed there instead of hanging out waiting for my father to show up at Álvaro's.

Sometimes while I waited—if I didn't wait for my father there, he'd get upset—I sat by the pop machine and did homework. Most of the time I watched the men work. Their stained uniforms and boots were the color of crows' feathers. They walked up and down the lanes, between the cars, a silver wink of wrenches in their back pockets. Eladio, Bruno, and Cheo were always talking loud about "look at this" and "look at that," never enough to rouse my interest.

All exiles, these men. They arrived from Cuba and came all the way here to Los Angeles. Most said they came to California for the work.

Álvaro's son, Alvarito, made me look up from reading because he was always calling me names, flicking gobs of grease my way, and I kept ducking them. A couple of times he got me, and I didn't find out until I got home and it was too late.

"Pedito," he'd called out to me, "Pedote." I hated it when he called me a fart, and he knew it.

I wanted to call him Captain Hook because of his short little arm and little white hand with the pudgy fingers, but I always held back because he was bigger than me and he had those screwdrivers and hammers at arm's reach. He wasn't that tall, maybe five-seven, and I was getting to be five-six, so I always thought I could take him, but the one arm on him looked strong. The biceps of his good arm looked pumped, and he'd put the little red-devil tattoo on it as if to draw attention away from his little arm and hand.

I asked my father about Álvaro's son one day.

"What about him?" my father said and wiped his forehead with the back of his hand because he too would hear it from my mother if he got grease on his shirt.

"His arm," I said. "How did it happen?"

"Ask your mother," he said and turned the radio on. "She knows the name of the medicine the mother took."

A bit confused, I sank in the hot leather of my father's Dodge Dart. Why should I ask my mother? Why would she know?

My father bought this car when we first arrived in Los Angeles from Miami and Cuba before that. He bought it for $500, and my mother hated the car because she said it wasted too much money in gas, and my father kept taking it to Álvaro's garage to fix this or that. I think the honest truth was that she hated for my father to go to that shop.

They were all Cuban men who were up to no good, she always told my father. All that talk about exile, what they lost, what they were back home, what they had. She didn't want to hear any of it. She was tired of the stories. But my father didn't listen, and he claimed that the shop was the perfect place to pick me up because it was between the school and the factory where he worked as a pattern cutter.

One day when I finally asked my mother about Álvaro's son's arm and hand, she didn't know what I was talking about. She kept asking me to describe it.

"I don't know," I said. "It looks like a little hand stuck to a little arm."

She paged through the telephone directory, looking for the address of a meat market she'd heard about. "*Sí*," she kept saying, "*¿y qué más?*"

I described Alvarito's hand as best as I could. I even made an analogy to his thick fingers looking like the little plantains my father brought home, these sweet, tiny plantains. Like the ones in Cuba.

"'Apá said I could ask you, and that you'd know."

"How should I know? It sounds like he was born like that."

"Some medicine, my father mentioned."

She stopped paging through the book and looked up at me. "Oh, *ya sé*," she said and put her finger to her lips to wet its tip again to turn the pages easier. "*Talidomina*."

"T-A-L-I-D-O-M-I-N-A," she spelled it out in Spanish.

I asked what it was in English and she shrugged. "Ask one of your teachers."

I thought about the next time Alvarito was mean to me, I might just say the name of the medicine to him. See if that got him to lay off me.

And one day, while I waited at the garage, he kept harassing me about being a sissy, how I chose to play tennis at school instead of football or baseball, and how I kept reading my magazines and books. What was I, anyway, some kind of fairy? He said the word "fairy," but it sounded like "furry."

Alvarito had dropped out of high school, and his father made him work in the garage to cover his expenses—in particular, the fixing up of a convertible Mustang he bought from a junkyard and was working on piece by piece. With the one good hand, I thought.

So I asked him, point blank, if he knew what Talidomina was. He stopped in front of me, dirty sweat already on his tanned face, a couple of scratches and bumps on his cheeks. He looked at me with his coal-colored eyes, confused, almost absentmindedly wiping the porcelain of a spark plug.

"What the hell is that?" he asked.

"You know," I said, "the medicine."

"What medicine?"

I swallowed wrong and started to cough. If he didn't know, well . . . maybe I was pronouncing it wrong and maybe he only knew the pronunciation in English, and I didn't know what it was, in English.

"Look," he said, "are you sitting there thinking of something to say about my fucking arm?" He stopped and looked underneath a couple of the cars in the shop, as though he had dropped something.

"I can kick your ass with both of my arms tied behind my back, punk," he said and showed me his yellowed teeth.

I had never been scared of him before then, and suddenly I felt respect. The way he snarled at me like I'd seen dogs do to mail carriers. All yellow teeth, with saliva froth and all.

"I've heard it all," he said, and spat in front of my shoes. "All the shitty jokes, all my life."

I sat there sinking. Both feet flat on the ground. My hands moist against my pants.

"Thalidomide," he said, pronouncing it in English. "It's the luck of the cards. My mother took the fucking thing because a doctor prescribed it. There, see? And because she couldn't handle morning-fucking-sickness . . ."

I didn't know what morning sickness was and why anyone needed to take medicine for it. I felt dumb for not knowing. Suddenly, too, Alvarito looked vulnerable, pained.

"ALVARITO!" someone called from the other side of the shop.

"Coming," he said and reached over. I thought he was going to knock me out, but he merely tussled my hair. "It could have happened to you," he said and walked away.

I sat on that metal chair and felt hot, sweat beads running down the sides of my chest and back.

When my father came by to pick me up, I ran to the car and got in. I told him to take me straight home. He did. We drove in silence, though he kept asking me every once in a few miles if I heard that noise. The ticking coming from the left side of the car.

"I don't hear it," I said.

"I'm going to have to take it back in tomorrow."

And for days and afternoons to come, I would dread going back to Álvaro's garage, feeling like there was nothing left to say, and Alvarito would eventually stop working for his father, after a big fight, take off in his car, drive to Florida, never to be seen or heard from again. Almost the way I'd leave for graduate school, except I kept in touch with my parents, though I wanted not to live with them and their sad small lives.

That afternoon after we arrived home from Álvaro's garage, my parents got into an argument about the car repairs, how much money was spent on all the unnecessary work my father was having Álvaro do. I couldn't concentrate, their voices rising in waves beyond my bedroom door.

After dinner, I went to bed early, turned off all the lights. I closed my eyes to the shadows of the tree branches planted outside my window. I thought of Alvarito's arm, thick and short. I thought of his pink and grease-smudged fat fingers. The tiny nails with the dirt and grime underneath each of them. His little pinky hardly possessed any nail at all.

I thought of hands like that, wrapping around my neck, even in their smallness. Gripping, tightening, choking the breath out of me. Smothering my life out the way mechanics stub out cigarettes under heavy, oil-smeared boots.

Chosen

"Hear that?"

"What, Rafa?" Sebastián felt the burning behind his eyelids as he tried to open his eyes in the dark.

"The thunder, dummy, what else?"

"No."

. . . In the distance thunder rolled.

"Hear it now?" Rafael's voice sounded distant, hollow.

. . . "Yes," said Sebastián in the dark of the small bedroom he and an older brother shared. Shadows moved across the walls and ceiling. Tree branches clawed at the windows.

"Storm's coming."

They listened to the rain falling on the banana leaves outside by the window. It hadn't let up all night. It trickled from the sloped roofs and fell over everything.

"Is he gone for good?" Sebastián was referring to his father.

"Nah, he'll come back." His brother, Sebastián knew, was only saying his father would return just to cheer him up. This time he was gone for good. Their father had said so himself.

"He said he wouldn't."

"Wanna bet? Cowards always come back." Every time Sebastián thought he'd fallen asleep, Rafael broke the silence and spoke. His voice sounded so far away.

"I don't feel good," Sebastián said. His head pulsed at the temples. He thought of the dream before the storm started up.

He had stood in front of a chicken carcass riddled with maggots. He built up enough courage to turn it over with a stick, holding his hand over his nose and mouth. The heat made the stink of rotting flesh waft up to his nostrils. He didn't want to gag.

The maggots writhed between the sinew of flesh and bone, white slivers made whiter among so much reddened, bloody flesh. Sebastián thought of how the chicken had gotten there. Its headless corpse reminded him of a feather duster his mother used. When the wind picked up a bit, he brought his hand down from his mouth because he couldn't smell the rot anymore. He'd gotten used to it.

The chicken's feathers were speckled with dried blood. Some lay flattened against the purpled flesh, stuck there by the dried-up blood. When he turned the carcass over, a knot of maggots fell out and twisted like kite string on the dirt. Confused, the worms knitted themselves into a tighter ball.

Would they turn against each other and eat each other? Sebastián thought. He'd seen this before, the times he'd gone with his father to the cockfights. One man in particular, whose name he couldn't remember, had shown him where they disposed of the dead roosters who'd lost and gotten killed. The man took him there and showed him the mound of bones, the carcasses, the green-backed flies buzzing over the pile. Sebastián heard the Z-z in his ears for days.

In his dream, the chicken came alive, headless, its bloody neck stump like a broken branch. It clawed at the earth. It scratched something there in the moist ground. But Sebastián couldn't read the word. He got spooked and in the dream tried to step on the chicken, mash it back into the land of the dead.

Thunder broke again in the distance . . .

The rain had come in the afternoon, Sebastián remembered, when the clouds gathered and turned mean-looking with the color of lead. Gusts of wind carried dried leaves across the patio floor, hinged them against cracks and crevices. He watched the sky from the patio where he had gone the minute his father started to shout at his mother.

They argued about the same thing: when was his father going to stop coming home so late? Sebastián's father gambled away all his money. The family's money. He couldn't help it, he repeated whenever Gris worked him into a corner. Rigo spent all his time at the fighting cock pits in Matanzas.

Sebastián stood on the patio among the empty clotheslines and nervous chickens in their wooden milk-bottle crates turned into cages, among the rusty bicycle frames and mildewy box-spring mattresses and discarded stoves, among the pungent smells of chicken shit and gasoline and oil. He stood there in the rain getting soaked. He cried. The rain fell at an angle, so the roof ledge couldn't serve as shelter.

The rain mixed with the spilled gasoline, forming these gorgeous iridescent rainbows that swirled and broke with every drop. The water felt warm as it soaked his short-sleeve shirt and torn pants, which were made out of flour-sack yute.

Sebastián leaned against the lime wall and remembered what his older brother Brito had told him once: a man didn't cry, and if little Sebastián was a real man, he wouldn't be crying like a girl all the time, like his sister Kenya. He stood in the rain and remembered, and for some reason all he was able to recall were the bad times when he'd heard or seen his father, during violent moods, hurt his mother. It was something he'd seen three times already. His father hitting his mother on her back, on the side of her head. Her bruises shone on her face for days, turning purple, then black, a tinge of charcoal under her eyes.

On those nights, he was so afraid that he wet his bed, and then the bad dreams and all his bad feelings woke him. He'd clean up in the dark, by the window so he could see how to change, and then he climbed in bed with his mother.

Gris turned in fits, her flesh burning when it touched his. Her breathing softened as she fell deeper into sleep. Sebastián wedged himself into his mother's belly and breast, sideways, and rested his head on the pillow. He heard the beating of his own heart and mistook it for his blinking as he tried to see the shadows move across the wall in the dark.

Now the fever ran high. Sebastián's brother, who thought Sebastián had peed in the bed again, felt the high temperature on Sebastián's sweaty skin that night when they couldn't sleep because of the thunder. Lightning kept flashing into the room. Sebastián's flesh burned. Immediately, Rafa, as Sebastián called his brother Rafael, the last older brother to remain in the house, rushed to their mother's bedroom, woke her up, and told her about Sebastián's fever.

Gris awoke in a panic. She'd been dreaming of her mother again, falling off the horse and into the river. Drowning. Screaming.

She was a big-boned woman with large hips, but that night she sprang from her bed as swiftly as a cat might jump from a windowsill, ran to the bedroom, and felt Sebastián's forehead. Her hands felt cold to Sebastián. The heat on her boy's forehead and loins alarmed her. For an instant she was lost and confused, standing there in the dark of the boys' room.

When she pulled back on the bedsheets, she saw that the boy's legs were glistening with sweat. Right there between his legs, his testicles had swollen to the size of lemons. This, obviously, was not normal, she thought.

Alone, she didn't know whom to turn to. It was raining hard outside, so hard that the drops hitting the tin roof of the tool shack next door sounded like the gallop of horses. Death was coming for her boy, she thought, riding on her black stallion.

Then she thought of the only person in the barrio who could help her. Josefa the healer, the *curandera*, the medicine and herb woman—*la yerbera,* as people in the neighborhood called the ancient apothecary. But Josefa was too old to make house calls, especially so late at night and in such bad weather.

Time was too important, and Sebastián's mother could not waste it on what ifs—her mother had told her once that high temperatures can be lowered by bathing the boy in ice-cold water and alcohol. Home remedies passed from one generation to another, but she didn't want to deplete her chances. Where could she find ice this time of the night?

What if . . . Josefa, indeed, was the only one who could help her.

She wrapped Sebastián in several sheets and blankets and towels, anything she could find, and took her delirious son. Fever burned in his glazed green eyes. Heavy-lidded, the boy made quick, jerky movements, as if convulsing, with his arms and legs. He uttered some kind of nonsense spoken too softly for her to be able to decipher.

Like a bird, Gris flew with her son held tight to her bosom out of her house to see Josefa. Guilt strapped around her legs. She could not move fast enough. She felt as if she were walking in knee-high mud. Years before, when she had gotten pregnant with Sebastián, she had gone to see Josefa about getting an abortion. The last thing she needed then was another child. Kenya wasn't even a year old. Josefa said she could not help Gris.

曾终终终终

With Sebastián in her arms, Gris tried her best not to stumble and fall.

It was the kind of mean night even dogs feared. Usually, the dogs in the neighborhood barked at every passerby, but tonight they hid in their doghouses. She hated those dogs because their owners let them loose and they barked at her whenever she went to the bodega to buy food.

She rushed by in silence, and silence was all she heard except for the sound of the rain falling everywhere. The drops of rain fell hard against her skull and shoulders and arms as she hurried up the darkened street. That son of a bitch, she cursed at Rigo. One day she was going to kill that bastard. Cut his balls off, she thought, and feed them to the dogs. From one mean son of a bitch to another.

The road to Josefa's house was muddy. Barefoot, Gris took her chances and tried hard not to trip. Her heels sank into the mud, and twice she lost her balance and fell, knees first. Nothing would stop her, not even the rain, from reaching Josefa's house.

Lightning flashed.

Josefa's place wasn't really a house but a shack built awkwardly on termite-ridden stilts. Slanted, it stood to one side of the hill behind the city's dumping grounds. The closer Gris came to the place, the more the sour smell of rotting things choked her. With the end of the blanket she'd wrapped Sebastián in, she covered her nose and mouth and tried not to breathe in that awful stink. She covered her son's face.

Gris reached the porch steps completely out of breath. The floorboards of the porch creaked under her weight. She feared they'd crack open and swallow her into the rat-and-vermin-infested cellar of Josefa's shack. On the door she knocked so hard she scraped her knuckles.

Josefa opened the door. She was holding a candle close to her face. The yellow reflection of the flame lit up her black face and made her eyes look like moons. Cataracts blinded Josefa.

"Oh, *mi santa* Josefa," Gris said. "*Ayúdame, mujer.* Sebastián's very sick."

"Calm down, *niña*," Josefa said, opening the door wider to

let the mother and child in. *See*, Josefa thought, *it wasn't a cat scratching on the door to be let in. Faculties intact, faculties intact . . . she was old but not that old. Changó be her guide.*

"I'm sorry to bother you this late . . ."

"Come," she said. "Bring the child to the back room."

Gris followed the glow of the candle to a back room that smelled faintly of jasmine.

Though Josefa was short and skinny, her shadow, thrown against the walls by the candle's flickering flame, looked tall and elongated. She walked slowly, her free hand stuck deep in the pocket of the robe she wore. Her feet made a scratching sound on the floor as she walked. Nobody knew how old Josefa was; rumor had it she was over a hundred years old.

In the dark, the walls took on a completely different appearance. They appeared not to be there at all. Gris looked for stars because she swore the walls themselves were the night sky, clear, deep dark, with stars pockmarking the corners.

Josefa lit more candles as she told Gris to place the boy on the floor in the middle of the room.

"Remove all the sheets and blankets," Josefa spoke with compassion. "Bring the boy out into the open. Gently. Let him breathe."

Gris did what Josefa said. She placed little Sebastián on the wood floor. So that he could be more comfortable, she bundled up one of the blankets into a pillow and placed it under his head. Sebastián's eyes were closed; sweat covered his delicate face and forehead.

"He's burning up," his mother said.

"Remove his clothes, too."

Gris told Josefa about the boy's swollen testicles. "I'm afraid, Josefa. If I lose . . ."

"Hush now."

Clothes off, Sebastián lay still on the floor. Gris caressed his face as if rubbing would bring the temperature down. She was no longer paying attention to Josefa, but praying for her boy. The Lord have mercy on her baby—he'd always been such a delicate boy.

Josefa opened a cabinet behind her and rummaged through drawers. She was looking for the right herbs and plants from which to make the potion she would rub over the boy's stomach. His being was being depleted; a mantilla-like darkness had fallen over it, was pressing it. Something cold, too, had taken over his warmth. Sebastián's belly was swollen and taut like the skin of a drum. She could only guess from the outward position of the boy's belly button what the problem was. The boy must have touched the aura of an animal killed by a *santero* for sacrificial purposes, killed with bad intentions.

As Josefa took leaves and powders, mashed and mixed them with her fingers in a small gourd, and added several drops of melted goat's fat, she asked Gris if the boy had behaved differently at some point in the day.

"He plays for hours in the back yard," she said. "I don't know. I've been having trouble with my husband. Sebastián hears us and thinks his father is going to leave us for good."

Wiping her hands on a towel she kept on a hook by the side of the cabinet, Josefa stood over the boy. The ointment was ready. She explained to Gris about Sebastián coming in contact with a dead animal that had been sacrificed with ill intentions, used to cause harm.

"Tell me he's not going to die."

Josefa didn't answer. The boy would not die, but he would never be the same. From the minute she rubbed the ointment over the center of his being, the boy would change. His spirit would no longer be the same, but summoned from a distant place, from another source. But Josefa, having been a mother herself, didn't want to disillusion the mother of the child. She carried the gourd, knelt, and placed it at the child's feet.

Josefa found blood on the boy's skin, rubbed it off with her fingertips, and showed it to Gris. "This is not the boy's blood," Josefa said, then noticed that Gris's knees were bleeding. Josefa gave her a towel to wipe the blood. The ointment, she knew from what she had learned long ago from her mother and grandmother, must not be contaminated. It had to be pure.

The *curandera's* dark hands were wrinkled, her skin rough, sandy, worn with use. She started to rub the oily substance outward from the boy's belly button. Once she reached the boy's temples, she stopped rubbing, spread his arms and legs out, and rested her hands over his heart. She put her ear to his chest. The boy had a strong heart, she thought, for its beating sounded like the gallop of spooked horses. Josefa put her mouth on the belly button and blew into it as if she were inflating a paper bag. Sebastián squirmed then. His hands and feet jerked.

Gris saw the tremor of the boy's eyes behind his eyelids.

"Hold him down," Josefa told his mother.

It was then that the mother felt the temperature decline. His skin broke out into a sweat. He opened his eyes and looked around, not scared or startled, but as if he'd lived in that room since birth.

Josefa moved away from Gris and the child, back to the cabinet, where she wiped the oil off her hands, opened the middle drawer, and removed a bottle of lotion. She uncapped the bottle and poured lotion over her hands. Then she began to shake her hands, sprinkling the lotion all over her body.

Despojo, *Changó*, *a cleansing of the spirit*. Josefa stood still with her eyes closed, her hands clenched.

Sebastián's spirit was purified, no longer taken over by the aura of the dead animal.

"Take him home and let him sleep," Josefa said. "In the morning mix a pinch of this with water."

Gris accepted a small envelope from Josefa. In the bag, Josefa told her, was a special kind of herb that would help protect the child from further harm.

"What do I owe you?" Gris asked.

"*Diez pesos*," said Josefa.

Gris asked for Josefa's forgiveness, for she didn't have that much money with her. Josefa told her not to worry, that Gris could bring her the money when she had it.

"The boy is no longer lost," Josefa said.

"How was he lost?"

"No aim. No direction. In his weakness he became susceptible to bad spirits."

Gris and Sebastián spent the night in another bedroom in Josefa's house. The storm passed in the early morning hours. The sun broke through the clouds. Gris awoke to the crowing of a rooster. Next to her, Sebastián was sound asleep. She picked up the boy and walked out of the room. Josefa was nowhere in the house, so Gris left.

How would she ever repay the *curandera*? Josefa had saved her son's life.

Mariposas negras: My Mother's Return to Cuba

When she arrived, she remembered the heat and splendor, the way a cloudless sky made her eyes water, an ocean so verdant blue that seabirds stood out like dots everywhere. The red dirt of her childhood games was still there.

In the little town of San Pablo, the cane fields grew tall as bamboo. Clapboard houses looked like shacks, like they hadn't been blown flat by hurricanes and renailed a half-dozen times.

People still drew water with buckets from the deep hillside wells. Most of the fruit trees from her childhood grew tall in people's patios. The people looked older, more weather-beaten, but then as islanders, what could they expect from their years in the sun?

Her mother, who'd died from an asthma attack, was not there.

Her father, almost one hundred years old, still roamed the countryside, inspecting the fields that were no longer his.

At night, while she held his hands, they watched the lit makeshift candles cast shadows on the walls. She remembered them dancing there from her childhood. The dead. The people gone from her life. The ones who never said good-bye.

At night, she dreamed of cattle, of horses, of the old house filled with the laughter of children, of people coming and going, of another life, rich and full, when time seemed capable of stopping.

At night, if she listened hard, she could still hear the bullfrogs out for crickets and roaches in the hallways, the thick dust of remembrance now falling over everything, like rain, like longing.

The ash of memory, the ash of old dreams.

The Day the Police Took My Father Away

That morning, a heavy downpour flooded the sidewalks on our street. I heard it rushing down the gutter to the corner sewer.

As was his habit, my father got up early, dressed in his khaki pants and work shirt, drank the *cafecito* my mother made, and took off for work. It was another day at the Hatuey Brewery, where he sat by a conveyor belt and inspected clean bottles in front of bright fluorescent light before the beer was poured into them.

My mother was dressing me and combing my hair, even though school had been canceled because of the bad weather. A knock at the door startled my grandmother from sleep in her room, which was at the front of the house.

She came in her pajamas and slippers to my parents' room and told my mother there was someone at the door, and my mother clasped her robe tight around her neck and chest.

I snuck up behind her when she opened the door, and the sound of the rain stormed like horses inside the house. Two men in uniform said good morning and asked if a certain civilian (they spoke my father's full name) lived here. My mother said yes, who wanted to know. They told her they were there to arrest my father for plotting against the state.

Being seven, I didn't know what they were talking about, but when the men turned around and walked back into the rain, my mother flew about the house getting dressed, putting on her shoes, hurrying because she knew they were going to get him at work. She wanted to be there, to go with my father wherever they were taking him.

When she left, I stayed with my grandmother in her room, where she kept her dentures in a glass of water.

We sat on her rocking chair by the open window waiting for daylight (there had been a blackout the night before and the power had not returned) as she read to me my favorite story out of her Harvard edition of *A Thousand and One Arabian Nights*. She tried her best to disguise her own worries and nervousness as she read about Ali Baba and the Forty Thieves, about the cave that could only open if you said "Open Sesame!"

The rain fell hard on the roof, relentless against the plantain fronds, which knocked against the window. My father was about to get arrested, and my grandmother and I sat in the half-lit room, where we had sat countless times before.

She read to me as best and as convincingly as she could in hopes that we would get lost in the fantasy of my favorite story: how rock can be coaxed into something soft and malleable, like a child's fear that his father would be killed.

Ricochet

I'm working the rubber band made from a long strip I cut from my bicycle tire's inner tube. The black, powdery residue of the rubber leaves fingerprints on the surface where I'm doing the work, trying not to get a tear in the rubber. This is the second time I try. I'm hiding in the backyard, by the sink and faucet, where my mother usually does the wash. Out of sight, nobody bothers me.

I'm thinking I'm going to have the meanest, best slingshot musket in the neighborhood. I'm going to shoot lizards' heads off with bottle caps. Fermín, my black friend at school, showed me the original drawing of the thing itself. I copied it, and now I'm building it back here by the chicken coops, using my father's hammer, scissors, and a few furniture tacks I removed from the bottom of the sofa. Nobody will miss them, and nobody can see the flap of material hanging loose like a dog's ear.

The rubber holds, dangles around my hands like a pair of black snakes. Fine rubber. The best, which I took from the front wheel of my bicycle. I put the tire back on so my father wouldn't see the tube missing. Only a flat tire, and any bike can have that. I just won't ride it, and if they ask me to, I'll say I don't feel like it. My father has been gone for two or three days now. The secret police, as my mother called the two civilian-dressed men, came and arrested my father. I'm here in the house with my grandmother. I haven't seen my parents in a few days.

The G-Dos, secret police, came for my dissident father. My father, the *gusano*—this much I know is true.

83

Every time I glance over at my bicycle with its flat front tire, leaning against the gate that separates the chickens from the rabbits, I think of my father. He waited in line for days to get me this bicycle, and I know he'll be angry if he ever finds out. My grandmother tells me he'll be back home any minute now, but we haven't heard from him or my mother. The neighbors keep coming by to talk to my grandmother, to find out what happened. When Miriam, our next-door neighbor and her son Chichi come by, I almost show Chichi my slingshot musket, but then I think better of it. If I show it around, everyone will ask questions. They will take in its beauty soon enough.

It's almost done, and I've collected enough bottle caps on the way home from school and back to have a real shoot-out war. Everyone in the neighborhood has slingshots, including Chichi, but nobody has this one. I hold the 2×2-inch piece of wood in my hand, feel its weight on my fingers. I sanded it down on the sides real smooth because I didn't want to get any more splinters in the tips of my fingers. I plan to paint it red or black, like a real pirate's musket I've seen on TV.

My grandmother, who cooks in the kitchen, keeps poking her head out of the kitchen entrance to ask if I need anything. I've been out here for a long time, long enough to get used to the thick, musky smell of the chickens. A rooster hops up to the fence and eyes me the way chickens do. Turns this side first, then the other. I aim the thing at it and pretend I slice its head off. One clean shot. I want to line up the trigger with the front muzzle. I've cut two feet of rubber for each side. I load one side, then the other. Each side holds three bottle-cap backups, so that I can reload real fast.

Then Ricardito, my friend from the other side of the cinder-block wall, shows up on top of the wall between his house and mine. I can't hide the musket fast enough.

"What are you doing?" he asks and licks his lips. He always licks his lips when he's nervous.

"Hey, not much." I want to tell him *not now*, that I don't want to play. But he looks like he isn't going to jump back down and leave me alone, so I glare up at him. He's older by two years, but I always beat him in everything we play. My mother once told me the story of how when I was three I peed in my bottle and gave it to Ricardito to drink, told him it was delicious orange juice. I don't remember doing it, but my mother says I did.

"Wanna play ball?" he says, his dirty hands gripping the cement at the top of the cinder-block wall. His father always threatens to stick broken pieces of bottles up there so we won't climb on the wall so often. Ricardito broke his arm once when we used to walk it up and down, balancing ourselves up there like tightrope acrobats.

"Not right now."

"Has your father come back?"

My father, the traitor. My father, the counterrevolutionary.

"No, not yet."

I feel the rubber band underneath my thighs as I squat over them so Ricardito won't see them. He's my best friend, but once he sees something of mine, he can't stop asking questions.

"My father says they can keep him in prison for good," he says.

I don't want to think about my father, so I don't say anything.

"They'll make him cut sugarcane."

Once you get him going, he can never stop. There's no way to do it unless you get his mind off on something else. I don't, because I don't want him to start asking me questions about what I'm doing.

He sits there and dangles his legs over the side. His scuffed shoes scrape against the cement. I can see the worn sole on one shoe and the crack in the other. He isn't wearing socks, and his

ankles and calves are riddled with mosquito bites, whole con-
stellations of them, some red, others crusted over with purple
scabs. The sores never go away because he loves to pick off the
scabs and look at them real close. He told me once that he
saves them all in a jar, and I believe him. I believe anything he
says when it concerns his body.

One time when we were alone in his house, he called me
into the bathroom where I had found him with a bloody mouth.
He kept spitting up blood and saliva. When I asked him what
had happened, he showed me his loose tooth. He'd pulled on a
tooth long enough to jiggle it loose, and now his gums were
bleeding. This was a permanent tooth, too; his father beat him
silly because of it. Now whenever he smiles, his gap shows.
His parents refuse to take him to the dentist.

"What are you going to do if your father doesn't come
back?" Ricardito asked.

"He'll come back."

"Not if they don't want him to. You think they'll kill him?"

"My grandmother says he will."

Ricardito hates my grandmother because she always chases him away with a broom. She calls him the little animal, the
little pest. "*Animalito*," she screams at him. "*¡Sal de aquí!
¡Vete ya!*"

He sticks his big, candy-stained tongue out at her.

Once he fell as he ran and scraped his knees, but he didn't
cry. I thought of him that night, in bed, waiting for the blood to
dry, crust-up into giant scabs so he could start digging his dirty
nails underneath. He says that if you look at the underside of a
scab, you can see the patterns of skin as it heals, like when you
cut a tree down and count the rings to see how old the tree is.
Except his never heal. He bleeds onto his bedsheets, and his
mother never asks why, or where the blood comes from. His
mother can't see very well. She wears glasses thicker than the
bottoms of bottles.

When I realize Ricardito isn't going to go away, I figure I can ask him to get me something. I need a big nail for a trigger. "Does your father have a nail I can use?" I ask.

"What do you want a nail for?"

"I can't tell you. Does he have one?"

"He might. It depends."

"If you get me one, I will tell you."

He stares at me with his eyebrows furrowed, like he always does because half of the things I say he never believes, and also because he's too used to my fooling him and pulling his leg all the time. Maybe there's some truth to the bottle of my urine he drank.

No use. I see it in his eyes. He's in one of those lazy moods. I can tell. He doesn't feel like jumping down. What can I do?

"If I tell you what I'm doing, do you promise not to tell?"

"I might, might not."

"Come-mierda."

He looks hurt because he never likes it when I call him a shit-eater. I feel sorry for him all of a sudden.

"All right."

"Okay," he says.

"Can't you tell what it is?"

"A slingshot."

"Better than that."

"Where did you get the rubber bands?"

I didn't answer, just shrugged.

He jumps down now, his feet landing flat and square by the mound of bottle caps. He lands on it and crushes a few. Startled, the chickens flutter into a ruckus.

"Take it easy," I say. "Look where you're jumping."

He apologizes, but it's no use. I can tell. He wants to know more than ever what it is I'm building.

I show him. "See, it's a musket, a rifle, a machine gun of

bottle caps."

I explain how I plan to shoot bottle caps at lizards, at birds, at anything I find.

Already he's all hands. I hate that about him, his groping around with his dirty hands and fingernails. He's about to pull on the rubber bands, stretch them for the first time, and I yank them out of his hands.

If I find a nail, and I put the thing together, I can convince Ricardito to play firing squad. I heard Guillermo, one of my parents' friends, mention something about firing squads once. Guillermo never came home one afternoon. Guillermo was a *gusano*, as my parents always called him. *Gusano* means worm, maggot. I found out it means dissident, counterrevolutionary, the kind that could get you killed or disappeared in Cuba. When my father called Guillermo *gusano*, he always shot back: "It takes one to know one." And both he and my father laughed real hard.

I can play firing squad with Ricardito, yeah.

We look around the chicken coop and rabbit hutches until I find the right nail. Then I pull it out slowly. With one knee on the ground and Ricardito breathing over my head, I straighten it out. It has a wide enough head for what I need. The wide head holds the bottle cap under the pressure from the rubber band so I can flick it easy like flipping a coin up in the air.

I measure one last time, still making sure that Ricardito doesn't touch any more of the bottle caps, and hammer the nail into place.

"It's done," I say and hold up my brand new musket. "Look how beautiful."

"Can I hold it?" Ricardito licks his dry, cracked lips.

"Not yet," I say and turn away from him until I can load it properly.

The rubber bands stretch just fine, with plenty of tension. I imagine the bottle caps going fast and hard, easily lobbing off the head of any lizard, frog, snake. Great, I think and feel the excitement in my throat.

The rubber band hugs the first three caps, then I load the second one, another three. It's ready.

I want to shoot it before my grandmother hears us.

"Stand against the wall, just straight like that."

"Why?"

"Just do it," I tell him.

He backs up against the dirty lime walls in the patio of our house in Havana. A little nervous, he fidgets. His shoulders slump, his hands flutter about, in and out of his pockets.

"Move back more, right up against the wall."

Then I think of the perfect idea. I blindfold him to make it look real enough. Then Ricardito can't see, and he won't know how the thing works, and he'll be too scared to want to shoot it. I figure I can aim for his gut, or his hands.

I find a rag by the sink, take it and fold it over his eyes.

"I can't see," he says.

"That's the idea." I turn him a few times like he's going to beat up a *piñata* or pin the tail on the donkey.

Then I back him up against the wall. I decide now that since his eyes are covered, he won't have to face the wall. He won't know when I fire. He'll only hear and feel the bottle caps bite into his skin, and if I miss, he'll hear them buzz past his ears.

He stands there blindfolded, his head tilted upward as though he's trying to sneak a peek.

I walk back counting twenty paces. I hold my musket between my legs, pull back on the rubber bands, load, and aim.

"What is this called?"

"Firing squad," I say and close one eye.

I bite down on my tongue as I concentrate, all along thinking of the bottle caps as real bullets. The machine gun in my hand. Ricardito isn't my friend anymore, but my father. I hear my father's voice talking about how he wants to leave the country, take me out of it before the government brainwashes me into thinking my own father is my enemy.

My father, tall and thin, learns to study the bullet marks on the walls. He says they tell tragic stories. A whole calligraphic record of those who've been shot, disappeared, for telling the truth about corrupt governments.

I imagine an old-fashioned firing squad like the Spanish used with their shiny muskets. With their conquests. With all that rancor and rage in their hearts.

"What's taking so long?" Ricardo speaks and breaks my concentration.

I take aim. My trigger finger trembles against the nail, then steadies, and I open fire.

The Policeman's Story

After my father died in Miami, my uncle told me of how his brother saved him from prison or death by coming to the precinct station where both my uncle and father had served as beat cops in Old Havana.

After the Revolution had triumphed and Castro had arrived in Havana, chaos reigned everywhere and Batista's henchmen were being sought. My father, who always claimed he'd done nothing wrong, never beat up anybody or took bribes, borrowed a jeep from a friend and drove as fast as he could to Havana to find my uncle and get him to leave the station.

My uncle could not leave because he had a date with my aunt, his wife-to-be, and he wanted to surprise her that night. When my father came to get him, the city was jammed with people, cars, and trucks. All the world seemed to have gathered in the streets.

My uncle changed into civilian clothes and left on foot. My father finally found him in the old bar where they hung out. He was having a beer, listening to the radio, getting drunk because nothing would ever be the same for them, not for him, not for my father, because they were policemen. Our fate had been sealed as well: we'd all live in perpetual exile.

My father took my uncle to my aunt's house, where he sobered up on strong Cuban coffee. Then they both returned to my father's house in the barrio of Arroyo Naranjo, and my uncle worried that any minute now they'd come to get them. My father showed him how he had taken all the records he could find on them being policemen.

That night, they lit a bonfire in the backyard, smoked a couple of cigarettes, drank some firewater, and got drunk. Their mother, my grandmother, even celebrated with them, because she knew that her boys would find a way out of trouble; they would find a way out of their country, where they could once again attempt prosperity with their own hands.

Mangos

The mangos fall. Rot on the grass. Shadows pass over them when the afternoon storm clouds roll into the Miami skies. They lay eaten by ants, these red-orange orbs half-buried against the green stillness of the neighbors' yard. Feral flocks of Quaker parakeets come through, waddle over to the fallen fruit, riddle the mangos' flesh with beak marks. These gray-green birds stuff their crops and fly off to feed their young in some distant tree nest like the ones in the Baptist Hospital garden. Iguanas scurry from the croton bushes to nibble at the fruit, a dominant male holding his ground near the freshest-fallen.

At night, crickets quiet each time a mango thuds against the hard-packed earth under the tree. Or are all these creatures simply swarming for a sweet taste of the fruit? Even frogs cease to call out for rain, hidden in the V folds of palm trees and the plantain fronds by the sides of houses. In the mid-morning humid air, the mangos smell sickly sweet, even those mostly rotted through already.

This is Coral Gables, the old neighborhood where I grew up. It's amazing that this kind of tropical wildlife still exists here. I am mowing the backyard in a back-and-forth motion. The cuttings keep me dazed in the morning heat, while the mower's throttle vibrates in my hands. I count the fruit hanging closest to the fence. Lots of mangos. I bend over those fallen on my side, pick them up, and toss them into the shade of the fern bushes along the fence.

It's a small backyard, my mother's, so it's a quick job.

93

Even so, my shoulders feel sunburned already. Sweat covers my back, chest, and forearms. My hands still shake from the running engine.

I cut the engine, roll the mower up the side of the house and into the penumbra of the garage. I walk inside the coolness of the house, remove my clothes in the kitchen, and walk naked to the bathroom.

Damn heat, I think as I stand in front of the bathroom mirror, by the leak-stained basin, shaving in the single 40-watt bulb's dull light, cutting myself as I usually do from dragging the blade so close to the skin. The small birthmark on the left side of my jaw bleeds every time I cut too close to it, its trickle pink in the shaving foam.

Outside the window, I can see the mangos on the tree. They hang from a single thin stem, the fruit's weight bowing each branch. Most of the fruit is already ripe, reddened on the topside closest to the stem. In the afternoon sun they seem to glow. The faintest breeze claims a couple each time it blows. On the floor, fallen and littered about the trunk of the tree, they form a circle of softened, pockmarked fruit, in different stages of decomposition. Ants feast upon them, surely. It is the ants that attract the lizards. Chameleons flash the skin of their throats, inviting the females to take notice.

Flies, too, swarm around the fruit. These mangos support a whole ecosystem in the neighbor's yard. Mother's old neighbor, Dulce, who passed away a couple of years ago. Or was it last year? All of mother's recently dead friends and acquaintances—who can keep track of so many? My mother did. She did so as though she were keeping track of the score. As though she wanted to know how close death was drawing to her. All her friends. All her family now gone. She will be the last to die.

The house next door belonged to Dulce, a nice lady without much family. A Cuban woman herself who came to the United States before the Revolution in 1959. My mother always talked about Dulce. For the men and women of my mother's generation, history was divided into the *antes* and *despúes* of the Revolution. The before and after.

A young, attractive woman lives in that house now. She comes and goes dressed in high-powered business suits, skirts and matching blazers, drives a sporty Mazda, tends to come in and out too fast, her bumper scraping the sloped edge of the driveway.

She's early to rise and gets home at the same time every afternoon, her longish hair as neat as when she left in the morning. Sometimes she brings her briefcase out of the car, sometimes she doesn't.

In the afternoon she goes out for a walk dressed in sweatpants and a T-shirt, her hair tied into a ponytail. She returns home on the same side of the street she left. In the kitchen she cooks quickly, probably something out of a frozen box, eats alone while reading a magazine, walks up and down the hallway to answer the telephone. She washes the dishes while listening to a Cuban radio station, but she looks too young for that. She never looks up, never. I stand on my side of the glass sliding door that leads to the patio, which is right across from her kitchen window, and stare at her. But she never looks.

She's got the saddest look. Hers is the face of a woman who perhaps got married too young, divorced after a year or two, and now lives her days asking herself: What now?

In the middle of the night when she cannot sleep, she leaves the television on. The blue light flickers behind the curtains, flooding her living space, spilling out into the early-morning hours. Maybe she falls asleep on the couch. Maybe she dreams between fits of waking and falling asleep.

All the while the television snows light onto her face, her closed eyes.

I shave and think all I'm doing is projecting, though I myself never got married young, and am not divorced. My name is Rafael Ruiz, named after my father and my great grandfather, the Ruiz's of Oriente, Cuba. The Ruiz's of El Almacen Oriental fame, the market/*bodega* everyone knew. I remember pictures of my father and uncles standing in front of the place. My grandfather in his *guayabera* with an arm over each son.

Or the men and women, the *guajiros*, peasants, by the fruit stands in front of the market door. Mangos galore. *Mameyes. Guayabas. Guanábanas. Anones. Carambolas.* You name it, they had it.

When was that? *¿Antes?*

I've come to Miami from Boston to settle my mother's estate, this small pocket of land, this tiny stucco house filled with Mother's belongings. I've been in this house for too many days now, and I have not accomplished any packing. Several dozen boxes lay flat between a kitchen chair and a wall, folded neatly the way they come from Office Depot. It's overwhelming is what I think, all this stuff to pack, to discard, to throw away. I don't have the heart for it. I don't know, to be quite honest, where to begin.

Here I am, a divorce lawyer, a man too used to telling other people to divide things, split them up, sell everything, get out while they still can, and start their lives over again. The old stupid saying: It's never too late. Is it?

I should be used to all this by now, the coming and going, how people walk out for good. This country is full of gypsies. This culture of leaving. What helps me advise people on these matters has nothing to do with why I'm not packing my mother's life for a final time. It's not that at all. It's simply that by doing so, I'm packing bits and pieces of my own. Like these ceramic fish my parents picked up while on vacation in Mexico. They took a cruise and brought back so much junk with them. For days after that trip, my father glowed as he showed off all the little trinkets they bought: the stuffed *mariachi* frogs, those wall plates with images of Aztec pyramids, ashtrays, an apron, bottles of tequila they never opened or shared with friends.

I rinse the foam off my face, watch the white gobs of shaving cream and cut hair whirl down the drain. I step into the shower, open the squeaky faucets, and a spurt of cold water hits my back. It's not hot enough, and I don't care. I shower quickly, lathering first, then shampooing my hair. My shaved face stings with the shampoo. I put my head under the shower, close my eyes to the mildewed walls and ceiling. In no time, I'm done. I step out slowly, dry myself, wrap the towel around my waist, and walk into the cooler hallway of the darkening house.

Yellowed with age, the pictures are everywhere, hung behind dusty frames. My mother's collection in the hallways. She loved picture frames, I think, perhaps more than the pictures themselves.

I no longer have any connections to this place. Not a one, and the memories are few and far between, but those that linger refuse to let go. My old man talked to me about those mangos falling in the next-door neighbor's yard. Dulce would let him come over and knock down as many as he liked. He knocked down a couple of baskets for her, and she made marmalade, which she brought over in Tupperware containers for my father to eat. The old man had a sweet tooth. He ate the dessert with a wedge of cream cheese. He liked mangos like this, not as fruit, he said, because as fruit they didn't taste anything like the mangos in Cuba.

All Cubans are always saying that: nothing ever tastes as good, or as delicious, or as sweet as what they ate or grew in Cuba. It's what made my father charming, I think, and it's also what got to his heart in the end. My father died one afternoon watching a baseball game. He reached over for a glass and had a massive coronary. Died instantly, the paramedic said. Instantly equals painlessly, right?

I feel like a ghost here, like I'm the one who is absent. This house of hot rooms like crazy longing. I've been down here longer than I've needed to be. Sometimes I find it hard to breathe, and when I lay on the bed my parents slept in, under the air current of a ceiling fan, it's even harder. It seems this house doesn't carry air well. It's stuffy, heavy, old air. I opened the windows and Spanish music floats over from the house next door.

Sometimes I close my eyes. Sometimes I keep them open long after it has grown completely dark inside the room.

"It's your turn," my brother says on the phone from Atlanta, where he lives, "to handle this final matter." He's trying to disguise impatience in his voice by clearing his throat with a low guttural cough. At times he simply pronounces his words slowly.

I am the oldest of three. My sister came to stay with my mother during the last months of her illness.

Sarita came from Cleveland, where she helps her American husband, Daniel, run a Subway sandwich franchise. What they call a franchise, anyway, which to them is only two stores. She manages one, he the other. They never see each other, that's what I hear. She spends her days in the back office interviewing job applicants, firing them for doing things like putting too many olives in a sandwich. Everything is counted; everything is measured.

When my mother died, I flew from Boston. A bad day to fly all around. The plane took off almost vertically. The pilot said we had to take off like that because of the limited space. I thought it was the bad weather. Three hours later, still stormy,

I arrived in the Miami heat. The airport is not too far from where mother lived in the Gables.

We all gathered for the funeral, a quick affair at Caballero Funeral Home, the Cuban funeral home. Well, it was Cuban-owned and operated at one time, the time of my parents, when my father and mother were always getting dressed up to go to somebody's funeral. My father with his cuff-link collection. His silk ties. His *guayaberas* now hung in the closet inside their cleaner's plastic. They hang there, ghostly in their starched uselessness. Mother never threw anything out. After the old man died, she kept it all. Once she said she was going to pack it all and take it to the church so they would send it to Cuba, after last year's hurricane.

After the funeral, everyone returned to their own homes, to their own families, in their separate states. My brother, Frank, makes his home in Atlanta, not too far from the university where he teaches, and being the closest to Florida, he'd come often, then report on mother's condition, which worsened during a bout with pneumonia this summer.

It is the middle of July now. The heat is thick, and these old window-unit air conditioners don't circulate enough cool air.

"You've grown soft," my father would say each time I came home from college and I cut the lawn in spurts because I had to stop to drink cold water. I would stand on their porch and pant like a dog. He'd bring me lemonade my mother made extra sweet, lots of ice. The glass sweated in my hands while I gulped the lemonade down.

That wasn't so long ago, I think, and fill a glass with water. I have been down here now for five days. I don't know what to do, or rather where to start. My wife, Kate, has stopped calling. I call her now instead, when I think there's something new to tell her, but there is nothing, and I have to take little action to settle things. Where to begin? No forward momentum . . . Where to *fucki*ng begin?

I walk up and down the hallways thinking, my bare feet on the hardwood floors, a litany like the falling of the mangos in the neighbor's yard.

When my parents sold the old house, the big house where we all grew up in Kendall, my father bought this little house from an American woman who died. Her children sold it to my parents cheap. Real cheap. We'd come home and visit in this strange, small house of creaking floors, cracked walls that my father constantly caulked and repainted. The mildew grew in the bathrooms. If you only ran one window air unit, the rest of the house remained a sauna.

Miami's mugginess, who could take it for so long?

All the Cuban old folk are dying. I have a friend in Boston at the firm who keeps telling me that soon there won't be any Cubans left in Florida. That Disney will have to reinvent them— a "Cuba Land," magical, adventurous, rum and Coke ready. However, Castro's still in power. My entire life Castro has been in power. He has buried six American presidents except for Clinton, who'd be better off moving to and living in Europe. Only there might he get a chance to rest. All this trouble with women. Serves him right, Kate reminds me once in a while.

My mother's house is filled with the broken memories of our passing. Of our exiled lives, though none of us feels like an immigrant anymore. Or like we live in exile. We've become assimilated. We live in the mainstream of American society.

I shouldn't have come down. Kate advised me against it. She's American of Irish descent. We met in college. We got married soon after. We have no children. We like the simplicity of our lives in Boston. She took me to Boston after we graduated from law school, and I've stayed up there until now. My blood is now used to the cold. To snow.

Initially, it was hard to get used to the snow. There was too much everywhere. What a pain to get the car started, and while driving, not to slide and sideswipe another vehicle on the slippery roads. But like everything, I got used to the snow. I am used to it, all right. Which is the reason why this heat in Miami is doubly difficult to bear.

I am a stranger in this house, too. I walk in and out of these musty rooms, recognizing what I remember of my parents' lives as perpetual exiles. In the closet, the suitcases my parents brought over. Once my father tried to throw them out, and my mother got in his way, held on to the handles, and would not let him out the door.

"*¿Para qué tú quieres esta basura, vieja?*" he said and tugged at the suitcase. What would she want with this garbage?

My mother held on, yanked and pulled until he let go.

Or if he'd so much as touched them, she'd know. It was as if those suitcases were part of her flesh. If he tugged on them, she'd sense it, even from the kitchen.

Kate hasn't given me an ultimatum yet, but I know one is coming. Two days ago I spoke to Franky, so much silence and static on the line.

"What's taking so long, Rafa?" he asked.

"All this stuff," I said. A thick quiet. "They were great hoarders. When was the last time you looked in the garage? There are boxes from floor to ceiling."

"Shoot, hire somebody to come and clean the stuff out," he said. "There are companies that'll do that."

Frank the realist, the quicker-picker-upper. This is the same man who grins up at me in the picture frame across the way. He's eight in the picture, freckles on his face, his front teeth not halfway out.

"Listen, I'm the one who's down here. Give me a break."

"It's up to you, brother."

When he says "brother," Frank's old Miami accent still rings through, as in *bro-der*. It's the only trace of having lived down here. "You know how long you need to stay."

He is right, I think. I feel stuck to this wooden floor. My

feet make this tiny suction noise as I walk because of the sweat
I drip everywhere.

"I can't let all this stuff go. Some of it is valuable."

"Separate the good things, put them aside, take them with
you," Frank said and cleared his voice on the other end. "I certainly don't want anything. Mom already gave me what she
thought I should keep. Each time I went down, she loaded me
up."

"You didn't take enough," I told him.

"I took what she gave me. What she wanted me to have."

Probably mother pushed things on him, things he didn't
want anyway. He probably threw them out as soon as he got
back to Atlanta.

"There's pictures. Jewelry. Clothes."

I parted the curtains and looked out at the street. School
was out. It was hot, and the kids walking home from school
looked tired, dragging themselves home. No rain in the fore-
cast. Actually, it hadn't rained since I arrived.

"Do what I tell you," Frank said, "and call one of those
places."

I told him I'd look into it, all right. The phone book sat on
the telephone table in the kitchen by the door that led to the
garage. Yesterday, I walked in there. Replaced the burnt-out
bulb. All these boxes stacked up against the walls. A lifetime
of packing.

"You've been looking for a few days now. The sooner you
empty it out, the faster the realtor can put the house up for
sale."

We never lived here as kids; that's why none of us feels any
connection to this house. By the time my father and mother
moved in, we were on our own. None of us felt attachment. We
loved the old house in Kendall and thought fondly of our days
there. Its big yard where Frank and I played flag football with
our friends. We built a fort by a fallen tree in the back. We kept

Sara out. Boys only, we told her. My mother would chase us out and tell us if Sara couldn't be in there, neither could we.

Frank needed to go. We hung up. He hasn't called back. He probably thinks I've taken care of everything already, and I'm on my way back to Kate, to my life in Boston.

I sit on the old man's chair with the footrest, the one in which he suffered the coronary, and I look at the worn carpet. Everything looks Miami Beach cheap here. Or is it all the years past? The television console holds rows and rows of picture frames. Franky and I with our brand new Huffys the Christmas of 1972. Sarita with Mochito, her French poodle. She fed him pieces of chicken while he rested on his back. He ate that way—she trained him to. Chunk after chunk. He grew fat. When Sarita went away to school, my mother and father kept Mochito until he died of old age.

Faded black-and-whites of Franky's graduation, of Sarita's, mine from St. Brandon's. The three of us at college. I ended up at Louisiana State University. There's the one of me teasing Tony the tiger from outside his cage. Those years my parents spent going from college campus to college campus. They drove to LSU and back. To Sarita's and Franky's schools, they flew.

Had they not immigrated from Cuba, we could have easily believed we had lived in the United States all our lives. If our parents didn't speak Spanish to us, they could have fooled us. They could have made up the story of our being born and raised in the States. That simple.

I am sitting there on the chair when I hear a car's engine turn a couple of times and die. A door slams shut. A hood pops open. I get up and peek outside the window. It is the neighbor trying to get her car started.

I go to the bedroom, get dressed in a pair of shorts, put on a tight-fitting T-shirt, and my tennis shoes without socks. I hurry to the garage, where I remembered my father keeping his jumper cables. He hung them behind the kitchen/garage door. I grabbed them and walked outside.

She's trying to turn the engine, but it clearly sounds like the battery is dead.

Walking across the front lawn, I reach her in time before she gets out. She has on an electric-blue evening dress. There's a gold necklace around her neck, her nails are done. She's wearing makeup, red lipstick. Her hair is smoothed over her ears and tied in the back with a Spanish comb.

She notices my approach and smiles.

"I've got these," I tell her and hold up the cables.

She tries the engine one more time. Uncertainty is my business, I want to say, but don't because I'm already believing I'm a fool for doing this, coming out like this.

"It's the first time it does this," she says.

She starts to climb out when one of her shiny dark-blue pumps falls off. Her white, small feet slip back in. She smiles again. Her eyes are bright. She looks like a completely different person from the one behind the kitchen window.

"Hold on," I say and go to the rented car.

I climb in, start it, back it up, and pull up to the front of her car. I pop the rented's hood. Get out. Hook up the cables to her battery first, then to mine.

"Wait until I start it," I tell her.

"I know how it goes," she says. "I've had nothing but junkers before this one." She's smiling behind the windshield.

I turn the ignition, the car roars as I step on the gas.

A few seconds later, she starts hers. Nothing to it. I get out, unhook the cables, and absentmindedly throw them in the back seat of the rented car.

"Listen," she says, "thank you so much. You saved my evening."

"What are neighbors for?" I tell her and immediately feel ridiculous for putting it like that. I'm not her neighbor and she knows it.

She has never seen me before in her life. She doesn't stay up at night walking in the dark, staring at me across the way through her windows.

"What happened to Noemí?" she asks about my mother.

"She died," I tell her.

"Oh," she says. "I'm sorry."

The engine hums under the hood, sounding like it's getting plenty of juice from the recharged battery.

"She always loaned me magazines. She was a wonderful *vecina*. I'm sorry."

Her Spanish rolls off her tongue. *Vecina*. Neighbor.

"My sister was with her." And I want to tell this woman my mother died in her sleep, her lungs out of air.

We stand in the sun, and I feel the heat rising up from the cut grass. A thick vapor that wraps itself around my legs. Mosquitos bite the backs of my legs in tentative landings. She's simply beautiful, I think . . . her sad, deep-set eyes.

"I've got to go," she says and climbs in.

I move up on the sidewalk, away from her car. She pulls out and drives away. I stay there long enough to watch her wave good-bye as she passes. The car's right blinker goes on before she turns for good at the corner.

When I park the rented car and get back inside, I hear the phone ringing. I reach it on the last ring. It's Kate. I'm out of breath. She tells me I'm out of breath.

"Running?" she says. She knows I don't run or exercise much.

I'm holding on to the receiver, feeling the sweat drops bead down the sides of my back. "No, I was outside," I tell her.

"Oh, I see. You hurried in," she says and I can hear her walking around in our own kitchen. She's got a long T-shirt on over the pajama pants that she's worn since college. She's wearing socks, too. Her long hair is wet from having taken a bath. She takes baths when I'm away. She showers when I'm home.

"When are you coming?" she asks quickly.

Is she eating? I imagine she's chewing a piece of bread, or her nails. She chews on her nails when she talks to friends on the phone.

"I don't know," I say and sit back down on my father's chair. The armrest fabric feels smooth, worn, thin from the years of use.

"They called from the office today," she says.

"What did they want?"

"They wanted to know what I knew . . ."

Don't tell them, I think, and put my feet up. They, too, are sweating. The mosquito bites welt on the back of my legs, on my ankles, begin to itch.

". . . When I thought you were coming home."

There's a pause. I can imagine Kate reaching for the jar of peanut butter, which she loves to eat by the spoonful.

"When do you think you'll be here?"

"I don't know," I tell her. "There's all this packing. It's endless." If she only knew that I haven't even started.

"A couple of days? Four? A week?"

"Kate, I don't know."

"Settle it with them. Next time I'm letting the machine answer," she says.

I don't respond. I let the silence buzz between us. "What's going on up there?" I ask.

"The usual. The Henrys have another dog. It barks all night. Keeps me awake."

"It's hot down here. The heat's what keeps me awake."

"How much longer, Ralph?" She knows I hate to be called Ralph, but she thinks she's being funny. I can tell she's nervous because she knows I don't know when I'm going back.

"A few more days," I tell her and sit up straight. "I'll be done in a few days."

She says she's spoken to Sara, my sister, and to Frank, and they are both concerned about why I'm taking so long.

"It's none of their goddamned business," I say.

"You know what you need to do," she says. "I'm here."

"I know that," I say.

"Good night," she says.

"It's afternoon down here," I tell her. It must be cloudy there, I think.

"Do whatever you need to do," she tells me in a fading voice as though she were moving the receiver away from her mouth, and hangs up.

I imagine my arrival at the house. I will walk in empty-handed, depleted from another emotionally draining flight. Leaves will have fallen over the roof of our house, hang from the gutters, bunches of them hugging the walkway to the front door. Inside the house there will be flowers on the dining-room table, magazines neatly stacked on a chair, car keys on top of the day's newspaper. I will call out Kate's name, and there will be no answer. She will not be home. She will not be there for a while. I will walk through the house like a stranger, looking into the rooms for the first time, wondering who it is that lives here.

Emptiness swallows me whole. Like here. Like now.

I get up, move about in my dead mother's house, walk to the kitchen for a glass of cold water. The ice maker in the refrigerator is broken, though there's ice in the tray. I turn the tray upside down on the counter, cracking the cubes out. I grab them and drop them into a glass, fill the glass with tap water, and it tastes terrible. A metallic taste. It's the ice. I dump it out and refill it with room temperature water. Better taste. Coolness is nowhere to be found.

It is evening now. No more sun. I strip in the heat, turn on all the air-conditioning units. They kick-start and hum. Rattle like a car's engine. *Junkers*, she had said in her young voice. *Junkers*.

I walk around in the dark. Across the way all the lights are off, too. The night darkens very still. There's a storm rolling in. A nasty one from the stillness in the hot air. Fronds cast shadows against the hallway lights.

How long has it been since I've eaten? My stomach growls. I can hear it churning. I feel as restless as the flickering shadows against the walls.

Now it begins to rain. I crack open one of the windows. Maybe the rain will cool everything down. When it pours, I close my eyes. I am thinking of something my father said about the way he ate mangos when he was a child in Cuba. That he'd eat them in the rain because then he didn't have to walk around with the sticky juices under his chin, neck, on his hands. It never made sense to me, the stuff about eating his mangos in the rain.

Thunder cracks in the distance. Lightning flashes in the room. I think about the distance between the sound of thunder and the lightning flash. How far, I wonder, how far. It is the middle of the night. It is raining. I cannot sleep in this house.

I get out of bed. I wish I smoked. I wish I drank. I walk in the darkness of my dead mother's house, my dead father's. It is pouring outside. Across in the neighbor's house, the kitchen light is on. It is a sad light, faint. Rain shines off her window glass. I wonder where the light comes from outside.

I open the sliding door and walk outside. The rain pelts my skin. It runs down my back. The fence that separates the neighbor's yard from my mother's house is not that tall. The mango tree branches almost reach the fence. I reach out to grab a mango, but I can't. I climb the fence, heaving up as I pull my weight.

I make it over. Step across to the tree. The fruit hangs low. I can feel my way around. I pull one, then another. My arms soon load up with wet mangos. I am walking back when one of these motion-sensor floodlights comes on.

I feel caught, a man driven by what he cannot have.

A man with an armload of stolen mangos.

I am surprising myself. Stuck, I freeze in the light. I will not say what I'm doing, where I'm going, wondering all along who's going to buy it, this, my story of why I've chosen to steal all this sweet, hard fruit.

Cosas Sinatra

My father believed the streets of Spain to be clean, the civil police in rare form as they stood straight and saluted when asked a question, or for directions, lost dogs, etc.

In Madrid I ate my first apple—actually, more like a dozen—and ended up with *un empacho,* as my mother called an upset stomach. I also ate grapes, cheese, liqueur-filled *bonbons*, potato chips, sardines, oysters . . .

There I saw the snow fall one year, millions of flecks as if out of a torn pillow. I flew kites from our twelve-story apartment balcony, rode the elevators as a joke to the *portero,* who, unknown to me at the time, kept his eyes on German nudie magazines (glossy-page flashes of pink to me) and who cared less if I rode the elevator or ran up the stairs.

I watched John Wayne movies with my father at the Candileja's Sunday matinee: *The Guns of Navarone* and *Cowboys*, two of my father's favorites, and I would say mine, too, because we watched them fourteen Sundays that one year. There was nothing bad, I confess, nothing like what made those German soldiers in the movie put their hands to their ears every time the huge guns blasted a shell at the ships on the horizon.

I played soccer at the park, and pinball when I went to the bars with my father, who loved *gambas al ajillo*, fried *chorizo*, and tap beer. He loved serrano ham, too, all that cholesterol food that turned our cheeks red.

My father's Spanish friends called it *fortaleza*, this ability to line one's stomach with good food and good wine. If the place had a jukebox, my father put in coins and played the songs he liked by Nat King Cole, Matt Monroe, and Frank Sinatra—most of the time it was Sinatra, though, whom he loved.

I remember the pinball machines and how when I coaxed them the wrong way, they shut off and flashed "Tilt." I didn't know what it meant, and my father said that "tilt" meant what Sinatra did on stage when his elegant, slim body moved real suave, cool, and his hands and fingers shook to the beat of each note and he had this way of turning.

I figured it mostly meant that I was having too much fun and then I'd pull the plug to reset the machine, and my father gave me more money to start playing all over again. And when the machine went quiet one more time, I heard my own breathing rise before the music coming from the corner, always the corner of those smoky, penumbra-ridden bars where my father drank with his friends, and from where I would walk home, numb in the cold, hands deep inside my empty pockets.

I walked home to tell my mother that my father would be home as soon as the songs ended and he drank the rest of his beer. I thought of nothing more, just the wind, cold, the way the old men sagged in their overcoats on park benches, the way my feet ached and the blisters on my fingers hurt from playing so much pinball when I should have been doing my homework.

Those songs Sinatra sang, those my father loved, stayed with me. I watched the snow fall quietly and settle on everything, like sepia dust falling backwards from the heavens, like these memories that have found a final, quiet form on a leaden sky, when everyone was alive and happy, no matter the weather, and even the snow seemed content to find its way to the earth.

Those were the days in Madrid, Spain, from 1970 to 1974, when snow and cold lingered in the air long enough for a father to speak about music, *la reconciliación de todas las cosas* Sinatra, after so many years, for a father, for a son.

Those are the songs that stay with us until the end.

Tin Can & Fruit Crate Art, or How My Grandmother Spent Her Final Days

My grandmother spent hours cutting out the labels, scissoring around the shapes of plums, pears and grapes. She'd create beautiful collages of fruit in bowls or horns-of-plenty, and she gave them away as gifts.

She had cigar boxes full of those labels, and I helped her pick and choose the ones we both liked. There was fruit on the labels I had never eaten: apples, pears, and plums. Those she said I'd get to eat when we went to live in the United States. When I asked when that would be, she'd say *"No sé. No sé."* She'd mention a visa, which was needed for us to leave the island. When I said that I didn't want to leave, she'd say that neither did she, but she was worried about what would happen to my father if we didn't.

My father had already been arrested twice for counterrevolutionary activities. My father, she said, had been a beat cop in Old Havana and a lot of people knew him, people who wanted to cause him ill.

I sat on my grandmother's bed and helped her arrange the cutout fruit on the pieces of cardboard she cut from boxes. Her room filled up with these collages.

One of my father's friends, who worked at a print shop, brought my grandmother several hundred sheets of Chinese prints of carp, tigers, egrets, flowers, and hummingbirds. When my grandmother saw those prints, her eyes watered because she knew now that her collages would be even more beautiful.

I felt lost in the intricacies of the inked lines, the colors, the drama in each setting. For months when I came home from school, I sat with my grandmother until it was dinnertime, lost to how she cut and pasted. My mother filled old mason jars with glue from rice and yucca starch she cooked.

While my grandmother cut and pasted, she told me the story of how the Chinese families had come to Cuba fleeing from Communist China, and how they had gotten stuck in Cuba. When I asked what Communism was, she pointed to a landscape rendering of a tiger stalking a pair of royal egrets wading on the banks of the river. She was only worried about my father, our family, not about what happened to governments, to politicians. Some days we put together, at most, a single collage.

I liked the ones of the emperors, the Buddha, the samurai, the red and yellow carp under the arched bridge of a garden's pond. My grandmother rearranged them so that they told a stronger story. She added more people, trees laden with fruit, delicious in color and arrangement, the way she said things were going to be in the United States, where she had visited as a young girl.

She called out the names of the large cities: New York, New Orleans, Chicago, and the names of these cities sounded as tantric to me as the names of the fruits I had never tasted.

The Monkey Story

My father visited us in Baton Rouge one weekend, and while there, he told Alexandria, my three-year-old daughter, the story of the monkey in Cuba. We'd eaten some jambalaya, drank some wine, and he sat on the swing of the porch with Alexandria next to him.

His voice came in through the open french doors to the living room, where I sat listening. While he worked at Lenin Park in Havana, where they were building the new zoo, my father became the caretaker of the lions and tigers. He fed them the meat of horses he and other men had slaughtered.

Among the animals was a friendly Capuchin monkey, black, with a white goatee, which the men called "Chivito." The monkey liked to play in the tree branches, and when the lions and tigers fed, it liked to dangle from the bars of the cage and tease the cats.

Every day, while the tigers ate, Chivito swung back and forth, and made faces at the big cats. The monkey was tied to a long chain that allowed him to get just so close.

One day, the men ran out of horses to feed the cats, and food was scarce. When the monkey climbed up on top of the cages, squatted and swung his arms around to get the tigers attention, it slipped and fell between the bars. Before it could recover its balance and climb back up, one tiger grabbed a leg and held the monkey, while another tiger bit the monkey down, decapitating it. They ate everything, including the head, which fell out of the collar. The cats tossed it around for a while

114

before the largest cat pawed it over to a corner, sat down with it, and chewed through skin, bones.

When my father went to check on Chivito, there wasn't a trace of him, only the loose chain dangling from the bars in a looping W.

Alexandria, who still didn't talk, sat there very still, a look of confusion in her eyes because my father had told her the story in Spanish, and whenever he said "*monito*" and "*tigres*" and "*leones*," she smiled.

My father went on to tell her that the story of the monkey was like the story of his life in the United States. This in between, this faltering and falling. Being torn to pieces by what he remembered, by what he wanted to forget.

There was so much more he wanted to forget, and memory would not let him. Like the story of Chivito's fall in Havana, when my father was still young, young enough to live through anything.

The Year the Moscow Circus Came to Havana

They pitched the tents on the grounds of Lenin Park, in the wind like a giant's green belly. We heard about it at school because the ringmaster, a man with a thick mustache and bushy eyebrows, came with a translator to tell us all about it. He wanted us to inform our parents.

My father took me despite coming home from work tired. We took our seats in the back rows because my father was a dissident, and, as such, we couldn't sit up front with the rest of my schoolmates.

The Russian clowns marched around the stage in glittering sequin uniforms, frowns on their painted faces, and make-believe AK-47s over their shoulders. The one-legged unicyclists teetered behind them, trying to keep from falling, for if they fell, they would get trampled upon by the elephants in their camouflaged banners that read *"Cuba y La Unión Soviética, ¡Patria o Muerte!"*

The big animals blew their trumpets, stormed about like tanks, defecated on the hay-covered floor, and sweepers in bumble-bee-striped uniforms swept up the paddies.

A lion tamer in tight general's pants whipped the big cats into a frenzied revolutionary song.

Jugglers tossed human heads up in the air, the heads, the ringmaster said, of Cuban dissidents (*gusanos*, like us). The tongue in each mouth stuck out in mock slobber. Each man had confessed too much, my father wanted to say.

My father carried me up high on his shoulders, tall and

116

proud. Above us the trapeze artists fell, plummeted, as though shot out of the air, one after another, like dead quail, fallen, broken, caught like big fish on the billowed safety net.

The crowds cheered when the riot police demonstrated their craft by releasing rainbow-colored canisters of tear gas, shouting in Russian for everyone to go home, *a la casa*.

At that moment, the armless tightrope walker lost his balance, grabbed onto the rope with his teeth. He bit hard, hanging on, while we all held our breaths, long enough for his heartbeat to thunder inside the tent. One of the clowns aimed and shot him down. After that, my father carried me back home in his arms.

I fell asleep listening to his heavy, quickened breathing, his heartbeats like the hooves of those mighty Russian elephants.

Water Songs

Ay, mira, nena, nena linda
Ay, a mí me gusta el tiempo de lluvia.
Cada vez que me acuerdo del ciclón.
Ay, mira nena linda, ven a ver que vacilón.
                    –from Miguel Matamoros's "El trío y el ciclón"
                    as sung by Elíades Ochoa and Cuarteto Patria

Most of my life has been predicated by water. *De agua soy y para agua voy.* This water from which rises a froth of days overexamined. Holy water, *agua santa, agua bendita, como dice mi mamá,* this water that refuses to fall from the sky. Water to drink. Water for rebirth, baptism, to cool the heat, quench a desert-dry thirst, fill the etched cracks upon the face of drought.

The *agua de violeta,* violet water cologne—my mother would splash it on me as a baby when she bathed me, and which later I was drawn to its hiding place by its aroma. I took swigs from it, and it burned in my mouth like bad words, its powerful taste lasting on my tongue. To me, it was *aguardiente,* firewater like moonshine, like bourbon, like the liquor I gravitated toward with a vampire's thirst.

I made my way through a few bottles of *agua de violeta* as well as my mother's perfumes and lotions, drinking them before she caught on that her son crawled around the place drinking her perfumes, her rubbing alcohol, my father's aftershave . . . the smell of rubbing alcohol making me dizzy with delight, its dragon's-fire breath giving my misdeeds away.

I don't know what lured me to it with such abandon other than that I always saw my mother use it on everything. She cleaned her vanity's mirror with it, the kitchen counter, the medicine-cabinet mirror. Its scent lingered in the air like the humidity outside, promising a downpour.

Water of my childhood. The smell of wet dirt, soaked asphalt, the decay among flowers and the coffee plants by the side of the neighbor's house. The way clouds broke open with thunder and lightning and water gushed out. It rushed down our street, taking with it pieces of wood, trash, paper propaganda, someone's red handkerchief. I made countless paper boats and snuck out of the house to float them in the tiny rivers and currents flowing down the street. White boats like white wishes for something to happen.

A memory of cranes deep in a marshland. The origami birds my grandmother taught me to make when I was six—we made them by the dozens. Onionskin paper birds lay in drawers, on top of the radio, in my crib. Lace-thin paper birds strung down from the ceiling, shiny, floating like dreams over my bed. Behind the gauzy filter of my mosquito net, I thought they were planes, like the planes I kept hearing about on Cuban radio, which claimed they kept dropping orange bombs over a place called Laos and Cambodia.

The world is surrounded by water. You look at a map and drown in its indigo hues. So much color hugging the continents. Currents of water coursing underneath the surface, caressing the earth into the bliss of erosion. The history of landlocked water. How lakes and rivers rip through maps, this cartography of water's desire to flow toward water, to join water, its salty, faraway cousin.

This meditation on water always carries me home. My personal maps of places, some discovered, some not. As a child, the only map I had seen was the map of the island of Cuba. *El cocodrilo*. The crocodile. *La llave*. The key. Names given to the place by its people. The skeleton of an island, a great sea monster, its hump bent a little toward its tail. It wasn't until many years later that I learned there were other countries in the world, other places that were not surrounded by water.

I remember the first time I saw the tip of Florida on the map, a giant's foot about to crush my *cocodrilo*. Bully, I thought. And at school they never showed us the United States, the place where the Yankee *imperialistas* lived. Would they ever invade my little island, this island in the Caribbean, *La perla de las antillas*, a Taíno's, Carib's and Siboney's paradise?

My father loved water almost as much as I do. He loved maps, too, their lines, symbols, the way greens bled into yellows, all surrounded by water. This opaline and turquoise ocean surrounded my little key-shaped island.

Water and paper birds. The dreams of a long-lived childhood. The stories my paternal grandmother Isabel read to me from books whose titles I no longer remember—a few I do, such as *One Thousand and One Arabian Nights*, *Twenty Thousand Leagues under the Sea,* and *The Count of Monte Cristo*. Books I would later hold in my hands and close my eyes to remember Isabel's voice, the way her voice shook when she said *"¡Ábrete, Sésamo!"* or the way she pronounced the name of Scheherazade, who kept herself alive by telling the sultan a new story every night. Or Achilles, mighty warrior, and the secret weakness of his heels. Or Heracles who shot poisoned arrows at the Centaur Nessus. For years I thought my grandmother spoke another language, different from what my parents spoke.

My all-time favorite story, of course, was that of Odysseus, who fought the cyclops and who refused the advances of Circe and her potion that would have turned him into swine. Odysseus, king of Ithaca, who fought in the Trojan War. The Trojan horse story. Stories I don't think my grandmother had ever had the chance of retelling until I was born and she held me and rocked me to sleep in her chair. Odysseus, with his bow and arrows. Odysseus, who makes it through the storm.

In my grandmother's words, Odysseus lived through many adventures, probably more than were actually in the text she read. The story of a man whose travels took him beyond known territory and into strange and dangerous lands. A great sailor who knew the water better than Neptune. Well, almost better.

Water, even in fairy tales, myth, fables . . . water to take us back. So much water to attract nymphs, satyrs, the Minotaur, Pan with his flute, and he, Narcissus, who lost himself in his own reflection upon the shimmering, onyx-gleam of a pond's surface.

To this day I have a weakness for water falling from the sky. It rained on the day I was born, so I've heard from my mother. It rained the day my first daughter, Alexandria, was born at Mercy Hospital in Miami, Florida. It rained the day my father died.

The sounds rain makes. Solitary, sad sounds, like drops falling on the fronds of the plantain plants my father grew by the side of our house, right outside my bedroom window in our house in Arroyo Naranjo. Water from the sky to hush the sound of crickets at night. Water from the sky to start the frogs croaking, beckoning for me to remember the way back home.

A tropical island where rain falls every day like clockwork. Rain to take us back, way back. There is meter and rhyme in the way rain falls. There is poetry in its slow, precipitated flutter against leaves, underbrush, the way it disappears into sandy soil. How many nights did I not hear it gallop like spooked horses on the tin roof of our chicken coop in Havana? What is it about its celestial Morse code only the dead learn to decipher?

My father collected gourds, out of which he made coffee cups and water decanters. He left them to cure in our backyard, and there, when it rained, they filled with rainwater. The sparrows came to bathe in them, drink from them.

There are cultures that have a multitude of words for rain. In Spanish, rain is "*lluvia*," and "*diluvio*" is deluge. Every rainfall is different, and only the earth is keeping track of the pattern. Poetry is the study of rain. In my book, poems should have an internal knowledge of rhythm and meter as if each letter in each word in each line were a drop of rain.

It is not raining today. It is spring in the place where I find myself now, remembering what the great Boricua poet Victor Hernández Cruz said once of his condition as an ethnic poet in the United States: "Geography is the history of my body."

My body yearns for water, the distant water of my childhood. It craves it now, like those downpours of my childhood in Havana of the not-so-long-ago, but more meaningful now that my history, everyone's, has plunged over the lip of this past century into the watery arms of a new millennium.

A raindrop holds the upside-down view of the world, hanging from the tip of a hibiscus flower, a vortex of light and shimmer, a known-world shone upside down. The way my father's face always looked askew in the bathroom mirror as I watched him shave. The sound of water flowing into the sink's drain as he moved the razor over his pale skin.

The view of a man looking down at his son. A tautology of spirit, I would say, this slim difference between a grown man and his son. A secret passing of shadows across the moist earth, cast by cumulus clouds bursting open in the great distance, raining down over water. Water joins water, and to witness this convergence, you must travel up the tributary to the source and mouth of a huge river. How all rivers have learned the way down toward the oceans is a testament to love, to those currents that pull us away and bring us back.

I remember my very first memory: my father and I riding the bus on the way to Patricio Lumumbe beach, a.k.a. Miramar Beach, home of the Miramar Yacht Club, a place my father, because of his economic standing and class, didn't have access to. This is past the Revolution in 1959.

My father took me to the beaches at Santa María, La Concha, and Patricio Lumumbe, named after the African militant martyr. The saying good-bye to my mother and ailing grandmother always made me nervous, the ride in a crowded bus, the stench of petroleum invading my well-being. The way over took forever, and the way back even longer, and often, I awoke to find myself in my bed, darkness glowing beyond my mosquito netting, a cool breeze flowing through an open window, the sound of frogs calling forth the rain.

There were nights of my childhood when I thought I had learned the language of rain. Words for emptiness, loneliness, solitude.

At the beach, my father always took me to one of those *cabaña*-type bathrooms to change, and I hesitated because I hated the way those bathrooms smelled. I hated their marked "*Caballeros,*" their scent of bleach, their stained whitewashed walls, and their cracked cement floors with huge gaping drains right in the middle.

Once I saw an earthworm wriggling there, pink, specked with tiny pieces of dirt, being eaten alive by ants. The dank, putrid smell of not-flushed toilets, piss all over the floors—too much for a boy of five or six. I always wore my rubber flip-flops, but I saw how men walked around naked and barefoot, tracking in sand.

My father changed quickly, then helped me change into my little swimming trunks, made by my mother who chose to stay home to care for my sick grandmother. Isabel, my white-haired grandmother, whom I called *agüe* for *abuela*. *Agua. Agüe.* What difference a vowel makes.

Sounds. Words. The sounds of words in Spanish. The sound of water. *Aguacero*, downpour. *Huracán*, the Taíno word for hurricane. *Ciclón*. Cyclone. I thought of cyclops and his ugly one-eyed ways.

I learned later that those trips to the beach kept my father from cracking up, giving up and doing something dangerous, such as joining some antirevolutionary group. Those trips to the beach would one day stop forever.

I remember best the tributaries in the cracked cement floors of those stinky bathrooms, of the old part of the city beginning to crumble. Buildings already in so much ruin, the rubble of our lives in Old Havana, in Calabazar, in Arroyo Naranjo.

Then again, *La Habana Vieja*, Old Havana, was one of the oldest cities in the hemisphere, and these ancient buildings looked it.

I remembered those beach bathrooms because they inflicted the idea of decay on me, of things and people wasting, becoming dust, ash—water. Only water saved us. Only water could cleanse our spirit, so my father, whom I assumed didn't like to be in those bathrooms any more than I did, took me out into sunshine. An outside so bright I closed my eyes for a bit, then opened them to sand, parasols, women and men, strangers all, sunning themselves on blankets or sitting down to face the ocean waves.

I liked to watch as my shadow, and my father's, followed us over the little mounds and undulations on the sand. Children kicked up sand on each other, or dug themselves into holes, or built castles. I liked castles. Castles reminded me of knights and princesses, of armor-clad soldiers in battle.

Then the sea, its green opalescence, its vermillion, magical hues of possibility, promise, color. Though I've always been afraid of going too deep into the ocean, I love water. I love the feel of sudsy water lapping at my feet, the cool wet of sand pushing through my toes. My father takes me into the water, holds me for a while. I don't think I yet know how to swim, so I hold on. He holds on. Strong arms, I see the line of demarcation on his skin from wearing short-sleeved shirts. My father's skin always smelled of sweat, musty work clothes he donned to work in breweries, slaughterhouses, factories—clothes and skin impregnated with that smell of a hard-day's work.

He takes me deeper. I know because I no longer can feel the sandy bottom. I see mercurial fish dart about, lightning flashes below the water. Beyond us on the horizon are these black barges with mounds of something. Several barges that look in the radiance and shimmer of the distance like pyramids.

"What is that?" I ask my father.

"*Erisos,*" he says. Sea urchins. Thousands of them. Millions.

"*¿Qué son?*"

He explains that sea urchins can stab your feet with their *punzas,* their stiletto-sharp needles, and then you have to run to the hospital. Some are poisonous, he believes. They gather them like this, dredged, and placed on the barges so that they die in the sun, so they don't reproduce or come back toward the beach, where people can get them stuck on the bottoms of their feet.

It makes no sense, but we are going deeper into the water. I can tell because now we are in a deeper hue of green. Something rubs against my legs. I think of big fish. I think of the times I've broken my mother's thermometers to play with drops of mercury. You put your finger on a bubble of mercury, and it sneaks away, or splits into tiny bubbles that then converge, reconnect, merge once again into a larger bubble.

"*Aquí,*" my father says, and lets go of me.

I am kicking my feet now, trying to keep my chin from going under water.

"*Patalea,*" he says, "and move your arms, too."

I kick faster. I wave my arms back and forth, staying afloat for a moment. I feel the currents of heat moving up and down my legs. My arms. There's a tickling on my back, the cool water.

"You have to learn to swim, son," my father is saying.

I am thinking of water, of this cool buoyancy around me. This world of crystal liquid that wants to pull me down if I stop moving my legs and arms.

Water gets in my mouth, its salt stinging on my lips, tongue, and the roof of my mouth. My father moves away, and I am trying not to grow desperate. He motions for me to follow him, do what he does. He swims a little away, and when I begin to say "*No me dejes, Papá*," water gets in my nose, chokes me. I feel its brash, rough saltiness scratch as it goes down my throat, as it enters my lungs, or what I think are my lungs.

I cough and go under. I see my own pale skin underwater. I see my father's legs like some strange growth in the distance, between my eyes and the water that holds him and me. The hairs on his legs move back and forth as if they've come alive.

How could I not think of one of my grandmother's stories about strange sea creatures, leviathans of the deep, bus-sized squids and octopuses with electric flash-dash tentacles that can pull you down to a creature of ravenous hunger?

When is he coming to the rescue? I ask myself, shutting my eyes, feeling the sting of the salt on them. He is not coming. I will drown. I will drown. I will drown in so much water.

Then I feel the tug of a current pull me deeper, and when my feet touch the sandy bottom, a rock—something hard—and when I open my eyes, I see that I am standing on the bottom, below water, and then the idea to spring up.

I see everything with a ghostly aura, the way light fractures and scatters on the sandy bottom of a beach.

I rocket skyward and break through the surface. When I open my eyes and catch my breath, my father's wet face is there. He is smiling: "*Así, así, cuando toques abajo te empujas tú mismo hacia arriba.*"

He teaches me the one lesson that I still employ when I go

swimming and get tired, or get caught in an undertow. You don't fight the undertow, you go with it. You can go down, touch bottom, push yourself up, and move—a sort of walking under the surface.

"*Estás aprendiendo*," he says. I am learning.

It would be another ten to fifteen years before I really learned to swim without sinking, but it was a way to feel safer, as if I would never drown in so much water. It was a slow process. My father, try as he could to get away, would be followed by his only son.

I was terrified of being left behind.

I don't know how many of these beach excursions my father and I went on, but I remember them well because they were so different from any other times in our daily lives. We went to the beach on Saturdays. A few times. That was enough to make a lasting memory for me.

On the way back home on the bus, he would tell me once again how to stay afloat. It was like riding a bicycle underwater, he would say. People around us on the full bus would look at us, wet-haired, sunburned. They would know where we had been.

Sometimes I fell asleep on the way back, and I would not wake up until the next day, when perhaps the sound of thunder would awaken me, or the sound of water falling from the sky like the sound of a ten-thousand-man cavalry galloping in our front yard. And I would think the armor-clad soldiers had arrived to take me with them, claim the world of possibility.

Between so much water and poetry, the heart finds its rightful voice within a song. Between the living and the dead, this water song, a perfect *danzón* to dance to and remember the rain's alphabet for this Cuban boy's journey home.

Psalm of the Boy Cartographer

Geography is the history of my body.
                              —Victor Hernández Cruz

Your eyes already in the slant of drifting foam;
Your breath sealed by the ghosts I do not know:
Draw in your head and sleep the long way home.
                              —Hart Crane, Part V of "Voyages"

What is the secret of buoyancy? Lines?

He craves to know, out this far in the region where clouds' eyes water. Where his heart echoes, plunges, and rises beneath concave surfaces of these opaline waters, wreaths of kelp and seaweed tickle his feet.

What he remembers most is the path by which everything drowns. The sky a big wound, a tongue of fire that swallows the earth.

What rhythms carry in the silence? Words muted by a constant hiss of air, how salt dries and riddles tributaries of loss onto his burnt skin.

He remembers his mother's prayer to Santa Barbara, the Saint of Difficult Crossings, a chant-like murmur that carries him further than these currents of constant tug, pulling him into this recurring dream of rope, knots, how a quill pen catches on paper, fire from the mouth of the dead.

This upturned, upside-down world now drowns in memory.

What this boy will forever remember is his mother's litany to Changó, Changó Changó. A vastness of blue-green in the sea and sky, one huge mass of empty space, a silent geography of elements. How sharks rub themselves in mock caress against his dangling arms and feet, as though to say *we know you, we know your people*.

Out here where so much of history is ignored, those who suffer know. Those who are bound know. Those who are lost know. Those who learn to float know: this memory of rough sea, a nightmare of screaming in the night.

A boy, his dead mother, two countries between this ebb of hurt and pain.

Later, as a young man, he will arrive at the edge of water, plunge in, and swim homeward toward his mother. She will still be there, *abajo,* at the bottom of his sleep, waiting, her arms like welcoming tentacles to guide her boy home.

For Elián González

Biographical Note

Virgil Suárez was born in Havana, Cuba, in 1962. He is the author of four published novels: *Latin Jazz, The Cutter, Havana Thursdays,* and *Going Under,* and of a collection of short stories entitled *Welcome to the Oasis.* With his wife, Delia Poey, he has coedited two anthologies: *Iguana Dreams: New Latino Fiction* and *Little Havana Blues: A Contemporary Cuban-American Literature Anthology.* Most recently he has published an anthology of Latino poetry titled *Paper Dance,* coedited with Victor Hernández Cruz and Leroy V. Quintana, as well as his own collection of poetry and memoir titled *Spared Angola: Memories From a Cuban-American Childhood.* He is the author of six previous collections of poems: *You Come Singing, Garabato Poems, In the Republic of Longing, Palm Crows, Banyan,* and *Guide to the Blue Tongue.* His poetry, stories, and essays continue to appear in national and international reviews and journals, such as *The Kenyon Review, Event* (Canada), *Poetry London* (UK), *Frank* (France), *Ploughshares, Colorado Review, The Michigan Quarterly, The New England Review, The Massachusetts Review, The Mississippi Review,* and *Quarterly West.* He is the recipient of an individual artist grant for poetry from the National Endowment for the Arts and an individual artist grant from the Florida Arts Council. He divides his time between Miami and Tallahassee, where he lives with his wife and daughters and is professor of creative writing at Florida State University.